THE
Emotionally
ABUSED
WOMAN

Also by Beverly Engel:

The Right to Innocence
Encouragements for the Emotionally Abused Woman
Partners in Recovery
Divorcing a Parent
Raising Your Sexual Self-Esteem

THE
Emotionally
Abused
Woman

Overcoming
Destructive Patterns
and
Reclaiming Yourself

Beverly Engel, M.F.C.C.

Fawcett Columbine
New York

A Fawcett Columbine Book
Published by Ballantine Books
Copyright © 1990 by RGA Publishing Group, Inc., and Beverly Engel

http://www.randomhouse.com

This edition published by arrangement with Lowell House.

Library of Congress Catalog Card Number: 91-72893

ISBN: 0-449-90644-2

Manufactured in the United States of America

First Ballantine Books Edition: February 1992

20   19   18   17

This book is dedicated to the little girl and young woman inside of me who suffered for so long all alone and who so bravely overcame so much of the emotional abuse of her childhood.

Contents

Acknowledgments

I wish to thank the following people for their contribution to this book:

My continual gratitude and admiration go to Janice Gallagher for her constant faith in me, her honesty, her steadfast support, consistent graciousness, flexibility, and endless flow of ideas. I also want to express my appreciation for providing just enough direction without taking over the project and for allowing me to muddle through my own stuck places.

A special thanks to Patti Cohen for being incredibly efficient, helpful, and patient, and for always being gracious and cheerful whenever I call, no matter how busy she might be.

Patti McDermott for so generously offering her time and energy to read the first part of the book, for her wonderful suggestions, and for her continual interest in my writing projects.

Linda Riggs for ordering some excellent feedback about the first chapter and especially for her suggestions regarding the Selfless woman.

Mary Nadler for once again doing an excellent job of editing even though it was a "rush" job, and for greatly improving the text without changing the meaning.

Derek Gallagher for being clear and fair about deadlines, for his patience, and for doing an excellent job.

Lise Wood for her valuable marketing.

Jack Artenstein for being such a warm and "human" publisher and for being so enthusiastic about my books.

And everyone at Lowell House who continue to make writing books a pleasurable experience.

My Story

I am forty-two years old, a successful therapist with sixteen years of experience, and I have written three books. Yet at times I still feel like a wounded, unwanted child. This is because of the severe emotional abuse I received both as a child and as an adult from my mother. That abuse caused me to doubt my self, my perceptions, my abilities, and, most of all, my lovableness.

Although I was also sexually abused as a child, by three separate men, the emotional abuse and neglect I suffered have been the hardest for me to recover from. My mother emotionally abused me in many ways, but the most damaging aspect was her criticalness. Because she was so extremely critical of me, I grew up with very low self-esteem. I always felt less than other people and lacked confidence in my abilities. I felt awkward in my body and unsure of my words. While at times I covered up much of my discomfort with a false bravado and could fool other people, I could never fool myself. I always compared myself unfavorably with others. I always saw others as being better than I was, as having more and being happier.

Early on I tried to cover up my insecurity by being extremely polite and helpful. I gave away everything in my attempt to buy love—my possessions, my body, and my self. The best way I can describe just how desperate I was to be loved and accepted is to tell a story from my childhood.

When I was about six years old I found a large, pink quartz crystal in a riverbed. I had always loved pretty rocks, so when I found this beautiful rock I thought it was the most wonderful thing I had ever seen. I felt very lucky to have found it and I treasured it for years, taking it out to look at it often, being comforted by its cool, smooth texture.

When I was nine, we moved to a new neighborhood. As a way of getting attention from the other kids on the block, I brought out my crystal to show off. As all the kids admired my rock, I finally felt accepted and part of the group. Then someone suggested that we drop the crystal and break it in pieces so that everyone could have a piece of it. In my desperate attempt to be accepted, I dropped my beloved crystal on the street and gave away pieces of it to the other children. When it was over, all I had left was one little piece.

This incident was a perfect metaphor for my life. I continued to give away different parts of myself until I had very little left for myself. I took care of others' needs and was generous to a fault—but I didn't take care of my own needs.

Until I was finally able to fully recognize just how deprived, neglected, and abandoned I had been as a child, I was unable to recognize how much I was allowing myself to be emotionally abused as an adult. Until I faced the truth about my childhood and my mother, I continued to lie to myself about how big and strong I was as an adult. In reality, I was still a little child, allowing myself to be victimized by lovers, friends, and bosses.

As it is with many women who were emotionally abused as children, I built up a facade of being supercompetent, fearless, and powerful to hide the fact that I felt so inadequate, fearful, and small. I presented myself as the caretaker of others, the nurturer and the rescuer, to hide the fact that I was so in need of nurturing and help myself.

Because I was in denial about just how damaged I was, like most victims of emotional abuse I continued to allow others to abuse me. Because my self-esteem was so low, when I first started dating I felt as if I had to go out with anyone who asked me. As I got older I became involved with people who were very much like my mother and who abused me emotionally in much the same way that she had. I often surrounded myself with people who didn't respect or value me, who took advantage of my generosity, or who tried to control me and were as critical of me as my mother had been. I was grateful for whatever small kindness anyone bestowed on me, because I didn't feel I deserved anything better and because I was so used to being ignored, deprived, or taken for granted.

I also repeated the cycle of abuse in other ways. I became as emotionally abusive to myself as my mother had been to me by not valuing and respecting my emotions and by not giving myself credit for my accomplishments. Totally disregarding my own wishes and desires, I forced myself to do things that I didn't want to do because I thought I *should* do them. This included everything from being polite to people that I knew gossiped behind my back to being sweet, childlike, and ultrafeminine when dealing with authority figures. I criticized myself relentlessly, expecting myself to be superhuman in terms of what I accomplished and of being understanding and giving to others.

I was also critical of others. Because I had been raised with such extreme criticism and very little praise, I tended to expect too much of others and have very little tolerance in my intimate relationships.

The scars of emotional abuse are still with me, as they are with all women who were emotionally abused as children. But I have discovered and developed a sense of self that I am now respectful of and true to. I have worked on building my self-esteem and on not expecting perfection of myself and of others. I don't have to be all good or all loving, and neither do the people I am close to. I have also learned to accept my limitations and to work with them in order to protect myself from further abuse as an adult. I consider it a privilege to share with you what I have learned about emotional abuse and its effects, as well as about how to recover from this devastating form of abuse.

UNDERSTANDING YOUR DESTRUCTIVE PATTERNS

The Emotionally Abused Woman

The emotionally abused woman is a particular type of woman, a woman who has established a pattern of continually being emotionally abused by those she is involved with, whether it be her lover or husband, her boss, her friends, her parents, her children, or her siblings. No matter how successful, how intelligent, or how attractive she is, she still feels "less than" other people. Despite perhaps having taken assertion-training classes, she still feels afraid to stand up for herself in her relationships and is still victimized by her low self-esteem, her fear of authority figures, or her need to be taken care of by others. She was emotionally abused as a child, but she may or may not recognize how extensively this kind of childhood abuse continues to affect her life.

> Sometimes I just hate myself. I don't know why, but I let everybody walk all over me—my boss, my husband, my kids, even my friends. I agree to do things I don't want to do, I go places I don't want to go, and all the while I resent it. I just can't bring myself to say no to people, no matter how hard I try.

> I can't believe I did it again! Each time I fall in love I think that *he* is the one, that I have finally found someone who will treat me with kindness and concern. But they all end up to be jerks who lie to me, use me, and end up not even caring about me. What's wrong with me that I keep doing this? Why can't I spot the loser, the jerk, instead of always being taken in? I'm thirty-seven years old, and yet when it comes to men I have the judgment of a teenager!

These words were spoken by women who have grown and changed in many significant ways. Nevertheless, they continue to choose partners and friends who cause them pain and embarrassment. They just cannot seem to stand up for themselves in relationships, no matter how hard they try. Because they have worked on themselves so much—through therapy, Twelve-Step programs, and/or self-help books—these women often feel hopeless and increasingly critical of themselves. They recognize that despite their efforts to change, there is still something very wrong with their ability to choose people who will treat them with respect and consideration.

It is often difficult for a woman to admit that she is indeed being emotionally abused, particularly if she is competent and successful in all other respects. But emotional abuse is nothing to be ashamed of. While it is hard to determine the exact number of women in the United States who are emotionally abused, we do know that the number is astronomical. While emotional abuse is probably the most common type of abuse, until now it has received the least attention. Many women who are being emotionally abused do not even realize what is happening to them. Many suffer from the effects of emotional abuse—depression, lack of motivation, confusion, difficulty concentrating or making decisions, low self-esteem, feelings of failure, worthlessness, and hopelessness, self-blame, and self-destructiveness—but do not understand what is causing these symptoms. Many women who seek help for their symptoms do so without any awareness of why they are suffering. This was the case with Maggie.

At our first session, she said to me, "I don't know why I'm here exactly, except that I've been feeling very depressed lately. I can't seem to get myself going. When I wake up in the morning, I just want to pull the covers over my head and go back to sleep. I have to drag myself out of bed and in to work. At night when I come home I want to curl up in bed right away, but I have to make dinner and clean the house and get ready for work the next day. By the time I get to bed I'm too tired to have sex with my husband. He's been complaining a lot lately because he thinks I don't love him."

"Do you love him? Do you have a happy marriage?" I inquired, wondering whether there might be marital problems.

"I do love him, but I just feel so much pressure in my life that I can't take any more from him."

"How does he pressure you?"

"Well, it seems that I can't do anything right. I know I'm not a very good wife, but I'm under such pressure at work, and I feel so tired. I guess I just can't be there for him in the ways that he needs me to be."

Maggie wasn't being very specific about what her problems were, but as the weeks passed I discovered that her vague description of her husband's never being pleased with her was an extreme understatement. Her husband was tearing down her self-esteem daily by constantly complaining that she was a lousy cook and a terrible housekeeper, that she never wanted to listen to him talk about his day, that she never wanted to have sex, that she didn't love him.

As Maggie opened up and shared more about her situation with me, it became more and more evident that she was trapped in a vicious cycle. The more her husband complained about her, the more depressed she became, the less energy she had, and the less desire she had to have sex with her husband. This made him complain all the more. Even though Maggie was not being physically abused by her husband, the emotional abuse she sustained from him was damaging her just as much as if she were being beaten.

Maggie was also being emotionally abused by her boss. An extremely demanding man, he complained constantly that Maggie was not doing her job. He verbally berated her in front of other employees, stood over her to scrutinize her work, and docked her pay when she was even a few minutes late coming back from lunch (even though he often insisted that she work late, with no overtime pay).

No wonder Maggie was depressed! It was amazing that she was even able to continue functioning at all with the pressure she was under. By the time she finally came in to see me, her self-esteem was incredibly low, and she truly believed that she was a lazy, no-good person who didn't deserve either her job or her husband.

The saddest part about Maggie's case was that she didn't think she was being abused at all, even after I told her I believed she was. "But my husband and my boss can't both be wrong," she protested. "It *must* be me—why else would they both be saying the same things? I *am* lazy, and I don't do the best I could at home or at work. I get confused easily, I can't make decisions, and half the time I seem to be in a daze. It's a miracle that I even do as well as I do."

Those who are being emotionally abused often grow to believe their abusers' accusations. The abused women do, indeed, become less and less productive, less motivated, less affectionate, and less sexual. And as their self-esteem plummets and their depression deepens, they also feel less loving.

Like Maggie and many other women, you may not know that you are being emotionally abused. While you may realize that your husband, boyfriend, or boss seems to be demanding and hard to please, you may not consider his behavior abusive. So what exactly *is* emotionally abusive behavior?

WHY EMOTIONAL ABUSE IS SO INSIDIOUS

First, let's define abuse. Abuse is any behavior that is designed to control and subjugate another human being through the use of fear, humiliation, and verbal or physical assaults. Emotional abuse is any kind of abuse that is emotional rather than physical in nature. It can include anything from verbal abuse and constant criticism to more subtle tactics, such as intimidation, manipulation, and refusal to ever be pleased.

Emotional abuse is like brainwashing in that it systematically wears away at the victim's self-confidence, sense of self-worth, trust in her perceptions, and self-concept. Whether it is done by constant berating and belittling, by intimidation, or under the guise of "guidance" or "teaching," the results are similar. Eventually, the recipient of the abuse loses all sense of self and all remnants of personal value. Emotional abuse cuts to the very core of a person, creating scars that may be far deeper and more lasting than physical ones. (In fact, a great proportion of the damage caused by physical or sexual abuse is emotional.)

With emotional abuse, the insults, the insinuations, the criticism, and the accusations slowly eat away the victim's self-esteem until she is incapable of judging the situation realistically. She has become so beaten down emotionally that she blames *herself* for the abuse. Her self-esteem is so low that she clings to her abuser.

While those who emotionally abuse others don't always intend to destroy those around them, they do set out to control them. And what better way to control someone than to make her doubt her perceptions? What better way than to cause her to have such low self-esteem that she becomes dependent on her abuser?

Emotional-abuse victims become so convinced they are worthless that they believe no one else could possibly want them. Therefore, they stay in abusive situations because they believe they have nowhere else to go. Their ultimate fear is that of being all alone. And, of course, the idea of being alone is extremely frightening to someone who doesn't have a good sense of self. For such a person, being alone means feeling like a child who is all alone in a cruel world with no one to turn to.

As noted, it is not uncommon for a woman to be emotionally abused by more than one person. This is because the pattern of abuse often started when she was a child, so she has grown up with low self-esteem and the expectation of being abused. As a result, she continually attracts abusive people into her life. While Maggie's abusers were men, not all emotional abusers are male. In fact, some women use other, less assertive women as targets for acting out their anger and rage. There are also misogynistic females—that is, women who have a deep dislike, distrust, and disdain for other women. And some women may be so envious and jealous of a female friend that they undermine and sabotage the friend's relationships or career.

Even though emotional abusers can be of either sex, most women reading this book will likely be concerned about their relationships with abusive boyfriends or husbands. Therefore, I will refer to the emotional abuser as "he" throughout unless I am specifically referring to a female abuser.

WOMEN AS VICTIMS

This book is written for women in particular, even though it is not uncommon for males to be victims of emotional abuse, especially as children. But boys who are emotionally abused, or who witness the emotional abuse of a parent, very often identify with the aggressor. They tend to emulate the behavior of the abusive person, thus repeating the cycle of abuse by becoming abusers themselves. This is because it is generally unacceptable in our society for a male to be seen as a victim. Males feel ashamed at being victimized and will prefer to be seen as an aggressor rather than expose their vulnerability. However, females are typically socialized to identify with victims. And since the role of victim is one that women are more accustomed to, they tend to tolerate abusive situations much longer than males do.

Maggie is a victim not just of her husband and her boss, but of society in general. Even though we may think that things have changed considerably since the women's movement began in the 1960s, the changes have primarily been in terms of increased career opportunities. When it comes to relationships and to who does what in the household, things haven't really changed much. Believing that cooking and housework are the woman's responsibility and that the man is the boss in the family, Maggie bought into her husband's complaints about her not being a good enough cook and housekeeper, instead of insisting that he pitch in and help. And, Maggie's belief in the superior position of men influenced the way she dealt with her boss. Because he was the boss and because he was a man, she believed that his wishes must be honored, no matter how unreasonable they might be.

In addition, many women are raised to be compliant and to "smooth things over" in relationships rather than to stand up for their own wishes and needs. They are much more likely to sacrifice their own needs if they think that doing so will benefit the relationship. These women tend to back down or apologize whenever there has been a disagreement, taking the blame for it.

Often, an emotionally abused woman feels compelled to stay in an abusive relationship because she feels a responsibility to her children. Even though her husband is emotionally abusive to her, she may continue to endure the abuse out of fear of not being able to provide for her children adequately on her own. She may rationalize this decision by convincing herself that since her husband is not abusing her physically, is not unfaithful, and brings home his check every payday, he is a good husband.

And single mothers with abusive bosses frequently have a very difficult time walking away from abusive situations, since they are often the sole breadwinners in their households.

ARE YOU BEING EMOTIONALLY ABUSED?

To determine whether or not you are being emotionally abused, you will need to work past any resistance you have to the idea, your continual doubting of yourself, and your tendency to give the abuser the benefit of the doubt. Even those women who already know they are being emotionally abused may go in and out of denial about just how damaging the abuse really is.

The following is a list of many of the types of emotional abuse that women suffer. You will readily recognize many of the behaviors on the list as abusive, but it may surprise you to discover some that you may not think of as abusive.

☐ Domination
☐ Verbal assaults
☐ Abusive expectations
☐ Emotional blackmail
☐ Unpredictable responses
☐ Constant criticism
☐ Character assassination
☐ Gaslighting
☐ Constant chaos
☐ Sexual harassment

Domination

People who dominate others need to be in charge, and they often try to control another person's every action. They have to have their own way, and they will often resort to threats to get it.

When you allow yourself to be dominated by someone else, you begin to lose respect for yourself, and you become silently enraged. Someone else is in control of your life, just as assuredly as if you were a slave doing what you were ordered to do. You are no longer the master of your own destiny.

Tia's husband Jim had control of all aspects of their lives. He regulated all money matters—how much money was spent, what it was spent on, and who had what to spend. Since Tia did not work outside the home, she had to rely on Jim to provide her with spending money.

> If I needed anything I would have to ask Jim for the money. This was always a major ordeal, since I had to justify my reasons for wanting it, and Jim would have to "think it over" before making his decision. I always felt like a child, asking my father for permission.

Jim also had control over the couple's social life:

> Jim was critical of all my girlfriends. He didn't want me to be around them—he said they were all whores because they went to bars. Instead, he wanted us to get together with his friends from work and their wives, but I had nothing in common with these people. The men would all stay in one room and drink and play poker, and the women would all sit in the living room with the kids, watching television. It just wasn't my idea of a good time, but I tried to go along with it to make him happy.
>
> He even complained when I went over to see my mother. He said that all I did over there was sit around and criticize him. I felt guilty when he said that, because it was partly true. But I needed someone to talk to. I'd felt so isolated since I'd married him.

Verbal Assaults

This set of behavior involves berating, belittling, criticizing, name calling, screaming, threatening, blaming, and using sarcasm and humiliation. This kind of abuse is extremely damaging to the victim's self-esteem and self-image. Just as assuredly as physical violence assaults the body, verbal abuse assaults the mind and spirit, causing wounds that are extremely difficult to heal. Not only is this kind of abuse demeaning, but it is frightening as well. When someone yells at us, we become afraid that they may also resort to physical violence.

Abusive Expectations

Here, the abuser places unreasonable demands on you, and you are expected to put aside everything to satisfy his needs. This abuser demonstrates a constant need for your undivided attention, demands frequent sex, or requires you to spend all of your free time with him. But no matter how much time or attention you give, it is never enough; this person can never be pleased, because there is always something more you could have done. You are subjected to constant criticism, and you are constantly berated because you don't fulfill all of this person's needs.

Melissa's father was extremely emotionally abusive to her when she was a child, and because of this she has very little to do with him. Whenever she does see him, he is suspicious, accusatory, and selfish. For example, as a physician he can well afford to pay her way through college, but he refuses to help her out financially in any way. Seemingly unaware of how much more difficult it is for young people to make it on their own today, he insists that since he was able to work his way through medical school, Melissa should be able to maintain an apartment, keep up a car, and pay her own way through college. As if it wasn't bad enough for Melissa to feel abandoned by her father financially, he remains very insensitive to how difficult it is for her and makes her feel bad that she isn't able to manage the way he thinks she should.

During a recent dinner conversation he asked her, "So, when are you going to start to college?" even though he knows that she doesn't have the money to go. Melissa answered, "Probably not for a long time. I hardly have enough money to get by on, much less save for college." At this, her father became visibly impatient with her and said, "Oh, I get so tired of your crying poor! You make a good salary. You're just waiting for me to finally break down and foot the bill. Well, let me tell you something, sister, you can wait until hell freezes over, because I will *never* pay your way through college! I had to work *my* way through college, and if you have any merit, you can do the same. There are no free rides."

After an evening with her father, Melissa always ends up doubting herself. As hard as she tries, she can't help but take in her father's words. She thinks to herself, "Maybe he's right— maybe I *am* just waiting for him to pay my way. Maybe if I really tried I could manage my money better and be able to afford college."

Emotional Blackmail

Emotional blackmail is one of the most powerful ways of manipulation. An emotional blackmailer either consciously or unconsciously coerces another person into doing what he wants by playing on that person's fear, guilt, or compassion. Women, in particular, are easily exploited because they tend to place others' wishes and feelings ahead of their own. They can be made to feel guilty simply for thinking of their own needs and feelings first.

You are being emotionally blackmailed when someone threatens to end a relationship if you don't give him what he wants, or when someone rejects you or distances himself from you until you give in to his demands. If others give you the "cold shoulder" whenever they are displeased with you, threaten to fire you if you don't do what they say, or use other fear tactics to get you under control, they are using the tactic of emotional blackmail.

Every time Mandy told her best friend, Gloria, that she didn't want to do something, Gloria became very distant and uncommunicative. This would immediately make Mandy uncomfortable, and she would ask Gloria what was wrong. "Oh, nothing," Gloria would answer, sighing. But Mandy knew that something *was* wrong, and she usually knew that what was wrong was that she hadn't agreed to do what Gloria wanted her to do. She resented Gloria's manipulation, but she couldn't stand the discomfort and pressure of Gloria's silence. Nine times out of ten, she'd end up agreeing to do whatever it was that Gloria wanted, just to break the silence.

Unpredictable Responses

In this type of abusive situation, the abuser has drastic mood swings or sudden emotional outbursts for no apparent reason, or gives inconsistent responses. Whenever someone in your life reacts very differently at different times to the same behavior from you, tells you one thing one day and the opposite the next, or frequently changes his mind (liking something you do one day, but hating it the next), you are being abused with unpredictable responses.

The reason this behavior is damaging is that it causes you to feel constantly on edge. You are always waiting for the other shoe to drop, and you can never know what is expected of you. You must remain hypervigilant, waiting for the abuser's next outburst or change of mood.

An alcoholic or a drug abuser is likely to be extremely unpredictable, exhibiting one personality when sober and a totally different one when intoxicated or high. Living with someone who is like this is tremendously demanding and anxiety provoking, causing the abused person to feel constantly frightened, unsettled, and off balance.

Constant Criticism

When someone is unrelentingly critical of you, always finds fault, and can never be pleased, it is the insidious nature and cumulative effects of the abuse that do the damage. Over time, this type of abuse eats away at your self-confidence and sense of self-worth, undermining any good feelings you have about yourself and about your accomplishments or achievements. Eventually, you become convinced that nothing you do is worthwhile, and you may feel like just giving up.

Character Assassination

Character assassination occurs when someone constantly blows your mistakes out of proportion; gossips about your past failures and mistakes and tells lies about you; humiliates, criticizes, or makes fun of you in front of others; and discounts your achievements. In addition to the pain this behavior causes you personally, character assassination can ruin your personal and professional reputation, causing you to lose lovers, friends, and jobs.

Amy was in love. She was engaged to a man she described as "the most wonderful man in the world." He was sensitive, intelligent, and good-looking, and he loved her madly. She couldn't wait to tell her best friend, Candice, all about him.

Candice seemed to be as excited about the news as Amy was, and she wanted to know all about Amy's fiancé. Amy felt very fortunate to have such a good friend, one who wanted her to be happy. Candice said she couldn't wait to meet Brad, so Amy arranged for the three of them to get together for dinner the next week.

They had a wonderful dinner, and everyone got along very well. But as soon as Amy excused herself to go to the ladies' room, Candice told Brad that there were some things about Amy's past that she thought he should know—namely, that Amy had been very promiscuous, that she had been addicted to cocaine, and that she had once had an abortion.

Fortunately, Amy had already told Brad about these things. He had reassured her that he still loved her, and that the past was the past. When Brad told Amy later on that night what Candice had done, Amy was horrified. She couldn't believe that Candice would have tried to ruin her relationship, especially since she knew Amy was so happy.

When Amy confronted Candice about the incident, Candice denied ever having said any of those things, and instead she accused Brad of trying to make trouble between the two friends. Fortunately, Amy knew better. She had always known Candice was somewhat jealous of her, but she never thought she would go to this extreme. As far as Amy was concerned, this was, unfortunately, the end of the friendship.

Gaslighting

This term comes from the movie of the same name, in which one character uses a variety of insidious techniques to make another character doubt her perceptions, her memory, and her very sanity. An abuser who does this may continually deny that certain events occurred or that he said something you both know was said, or by insinuating that you are exaggerating or lying. In this way, the abuser may be trying to gain control over you or to avoid responsibility for his own actions.

Constant Chaos

This type of abuse is characterized by continual upheavals and discord. The abuser may deliberately start arguments and be in constant conflict with others. He is likely to be "addicted to drama," since creating chaos creates excitement in crisis-oriented people. Seemingly unable to enjoy harmony and peace, the "chaotic person" bursts out with constant disruptions and negative moods.

Stella's boss, Abby, is always in a crisis. There is always a job that needs to get out "immediately," she is always in conflict with one of her employees, and she is always upset about money. Every week there is a staff meeting in which Abby spouts off about all of the problems in the company, making all present fearful of losing their jobs. The way she tells it, the company is always on the verge of bankruptcy or some other crisis. Not surprisingly, most of her employees are nervous wrecks because of the tension she creates in the office.

Sexual Harassment

Although this term is used most often with regard to work settings, a woman can be sexually harassed by anyone, including her husband. Sexual harassment is defined as unwelcome sexual advances or physical or verbal conduct of a sexual nature. Whenever a woman is pressured into becoming sexual against her will, whether it be because she doesn't choose that person as a sexual partner or because she does not feel like being sexual at the time, it is considered sexual harassment.

In order to be legally considered sexual harassment, the conduct must be tied to an employment decision, such as hiring or promotion, or it must interfere with work performance or create a hostile work environment.

In a recent L.A. Times article Charles H. Goldstein, narrator of a videotape entitled *How to Prevent Sexual-Harassment Lawsuits,* stated that sexual harassment is one of the most serious problems women face in the work force.

Even off-color jokes can constitute sexual harassment. Until very recently, it was simply considered part of the job to put up with off-color or sexist jokes, comments about one's body and one's real or imagined sex life, and even sexual propositions. Women often felt that if they did not at least tolerate such overtures, they might lose their jobs. As Mr. Goldstein explains, "Although sexual harassment has been outlawed in many places, some people regard the laws as unfair restrictions on fellows who are just out to make a joke or have a good time. Women who bring charges of sexual harassment against their employers are often regarded as bitches who are out to cramp men's style."

Olivia is a very attractive mother of three who is the sole support of her family. She worked long and hard to get her real estate license, and she was finally accepted into a prestigious real estate office. When she was hired, the owner of the office, George, promised that if she did well he would let more and more of the bigger accounts list with her.

When George told her he felt she would do well given that she was so attractive, she just let the remark go; she was used to having people make such comments. But it wasn't long before George started making sexual advances toward her. Because he did this in a breezy way that could be interpreted as "just kidding," Olivia responded in kind, turning him down in a joking way. But George mistook her joking for encouragement. He began to get bolder and bolder, making overtly sexual remarks and putting his arm around her whenever he got a chance. Olivia didn't want to offend George because she knew he was the one who determined what listings she got, so she continued to brush him off in a casual, joking kind of way.

At the staff Christmas party George cornered Olivia in the back of the office, held some mistletoe over her head, and insisted on a kiss. Feeling in the Christmas spirit, she gave him a quick kiss and tried to slip away. But George wasn't going to let her go so easily. He grabbed her and held her so tightly she couldn't get away, and he started rubbing his body up against hers and trying to touch her breasts. Luckily, another staff member walked into the room just then, and George let Olivia go.

After this, Olivia was really in a quandary. It was getting so that she was afraid to be around George because she thought he might make more advances. But because he was giving her some good accounts and promising to give her more, she convinced herself that she could handle George and that it was worth fending him off if it meant becoming successful.

Unfortunately, Olivia didn't realize how much George's sexual harassment was damaging her. She began to have frequent nightmares in which she was trapped, pinned down, or raped. The nightmares frightened her so much that she developed insomnia, and she also became more and more afraid to be alone with a man. Finally, in desperation, Olivia started therapy. Not only did she not link her symptoms to what was happening at work, but she did not even realize she was being sexually harassed. These insights led to still further ones, most notably that she had been sexually abused as a child by a teacher. When she became aware that she was being abused by George in much the same way as she had been by her teacher, she realized the importance of quitting her job.

We are all guilty of committing many of the above acts ourselves from time to time, as well as experiencing them from other people who are not generally abusive. When a relationship is not going well, there is usually a great deal of arguing and bickering, and either or both parties may resort to name calling, criticizing, and other behaviors that they normally would not be involved in. But there is a vast difference between name calling or criticizing in the heat of an argument and doing so on a day-to-day basis.

Similarly, constant complaining is not necessarily emotionally abusive unless it is destructive and the intent is to make the other person feel bad. For example, a husband who complains that the house isn't clean isn't necessarily being emotionally abusive. But if he constantly tells his wife that she is bad, lazy, inconsiderate, selfish, and so on because she does not clean the house, then he is being abusive.

True emotional abuse is distinguished by the following:

☐ It is constant, as opposed to occasional.

☐ The intent is to devalue and denigrate rather than to simply state a complaint.

☐ The intent is to dominate and control rather than to provide constructive criticism.

☐ The person has an *overall* attitude of disrespect toward you, rather than just not liking something specific that you are doing.

WHO ARE THE EMOTIONAL ABUSERS?

Emotionally Abusive Lovers and Mates

Emotionally abusive lovers and mates can cause tremendous damage to a woman's ego. They have our trust, our vulnerability, our hearts, and our bodies. Using a variety of tactics, an abusive husband or lover can damage a woman's self-esteem, make her doubt her desirability and hate her body, and break her heart.

It is incredibly painful to come to the recognition that someone you love and want desperately to believe loves you in return could actually be abusing you. Because of the feelings you have for him, it is especially difficult to recognize that you may be emotionally abused by your husband or lover. When we love someone we tend to make excuses for his behavior; we always want to give him the benefit of the doubt. This is especially true when the other person is good to us in other ways. This was the case with Samantha.

> I knew my husband was critical of me, but he could also be so good to me. No one ever treated me as well as he did when things were going his way. But when he was under pressure at work, he was horrible to me. He berated me constantly, finding fault in everything I did. I became a nervous wreck, waiting for the next round of complaints. My opinion of myself became so low that I actually

considered suicide. When he wasn't under pressure he treated me like a queen, and I felt great about myself, about him, and about our marriage.

Answering the following questions will help you to determine whether or not you are in an emotionally abusive love relationship. A "yes" answer to even half of these questions indicates that you are in an emotionally abusive love relationship.

- ☐ Do you feel like a child in the relationship, having to ask permission and apologizing for your behavior? Do you feel powerless and "less than" your lover or mate?

- ☐ Have you stopped seeing your friends and family? Does your lover or husband criticize your friends and family members? Did he complain so much when you saw them in the past that you finally stopped seeing them altogether so you wouldn't have to argue with him about it? Are you ashamed to see your friends or family because of your mate's abusive behavior, and because you're embarrassed at having put up with so much from him?

- ☐ Do you believe that you are to blame for your husband's or lover's problems? Do you feel you are mostly responsible for the problems with the relationship?

- ☐ Does your mate try to take advantage of you sexually or make unreasonable sexual demands on you?

- ☐ Does your lover's personality change when he drinks alcohol?

- ☐ Does your mate use "humor" to put you down or degrade you?

- ☐ Does he lack the ability to laugh at himself?

- ☐ Does he find it hard to apologize or to admit when he is wrong? Does he make excuses for his behavior or always blame others for his actions?

- ☐ Does he usually get his way in deciding when and where the two of you will go?

- ☐ Does he control or disapprove of your spending but seem to have no problems spending on himself?

Emotionally Abusive Bosses

Bosses and other authority figures can influence a woman's career and her very livelihood. Because of this, we tend to put up with behavior in work situations that we otherwise would not tolerate. As mentioned earlier, this is especially true with single mothers who must rely on their jobs to support not only themselves but their children as well. Even the most assertive of women will be reluctant to confront a boss about his or her abusive behavior when it may mean risking her children's security.

There is a vast difference between having a "disagreeable" boss, one who is sometimes difficult to deal with, and having an abusive one. Emotionally abusive bosses use their power and position to behave in totally unacceptable ways. They may become verbally abusive, overly demanding or critical, or make improper sexual advances. Their most powerful weapon is emotional blackmail. They may threaten you with the loss of your job, with a poor evaluation, or with the withholding of a raise or promotion. The basic message is, "You do what I say, or else." Some hold out a carrot of promotions, bonuses, and so on in order to keep their employees working for them even when the conditions are horribly oppressive.

It is not a coincidence, of course, that many bosses have a need to dominate and control other people. Because they have a need to have control over others, some people naturally gravitate to positions of authority. This is not to say that all bosses are emotionally abusive, but that for some, having power is a license to be abusive. One of the ways that male bosses abuse their power is by sexually harassing their female employees.

Both men and women can be abusive bosses. There are misogynists of both sexes, and bosses of either sex may feel threatened by female employees who are bright and ambitious. Jealous bosses may do everything in their power to sabotage the employee's success.

While female bosses can be emotionally abusive in many of the same ways that male bosses are, the reasons are sometimes different. Some female bosses have an excessive need to have control over other women. They relish being the boss or authority "in charge" of other women, and they often abuse this authority. Other female bosses may have a deep distrust of other women and may believe—ironically enough—that women "just can't do the job." Such women tend not to hire other women for positions of power or to recognize the achievements of those who do work for them.

Emotionally Abusive Coworkers

Although to a lesser degree than bosses, coworkers can also damage a woman's career. In fact, a great deal of our success or failure at work can often be attributed to whether or not we are accepted and respected by our coworkers.

Coworkers have been known to sabotage another employee's career by spreading nasty rumors about her in the office, by taking credit for her work, by complaining about her to the boss, by stealing her customers, and by turning others against her.

Coworkers can, of course, be male or female, and both sexes can be emotionally abusive. But surprisingly, most of my female clients have complained of being emotionally abused more by their *female* coworkers, and recent research shows that males actually tend to be more supportive and encouraging of their female coworkers than females are. The following situation is, unfortunately, not an uncommon example of what can happen when female coworkers become threatened by another woman's success.

Dana was a very attractive, intelligent young woman who was tremendously motivated to become successful. Only twenty-four years old, she was already the office manager for a large corporation. Because she was so pretty and young, the older women under her were tremendously threatened by her, so much so that they secretly began a campaign to get her fired. They started refusing to follow her orders, and they then spread the word throughout the office that she was an unreasonable tyrant who demanded much too much of them.

There was so much disruption in the office that the head of personnel finally began to interview each employee to discover the cause of the difficulty. One by one, each woman in the office reported that working under Dana was a hardship because she was so demanding. In the end, Dana was asked to leave the company, even though she tried desperately to convince personnel that her job had been sabotaged.

It was this devastating event that brought Dana into my office. She blamed herself for what had happened, thinking that somehow she had brought all this on herself. As we unraveled her history, we discovered that this kind of thing had happened to Dana quite a lot as a child and young adult, starting with her experience with an overly competitive mother.

Dana learned that because of her previous experiences, she viewed all women as potential abusers and kept herself alienated from them. This left a false impression of her being snobbish, when, in actuality, the opposite was true—she longed for other women to like her. She realized that she would have to try hard to befriend other women, since many would assume she was conceited because of her aloof manner, combined with her looks and intelligence.

Emotionally Abusive Parents

Parents, more than anyone else in a woman's life, have the ability and opportunity to emotionally devastate her. Any parent can be emotionally abusive and, in fact, most parents are from time to time. But the emotional abuse that we are referring to is not the occasional oversight, not the sporadic incidence of a parent becoming angry, distant, or tense with their child. We are talking about habitual behavior and patterns of interacting with children that cause permanent damage.

It has been said that a girl's mother will be the most important person in her life. She will certainly be the most influential. From her mother a girl will learn safety or fear, to love herself or to hate herself, to value others or take others for granted. From her mother she will learn to be intimate or detached, possessive or freedom-giving. And from her mother she will learn to be a mother herself. Most important, if a child's first intimate contact with another human being is emotionally abusive in nature, it will set the stage for all her future relationships. The nature of the mother-child bond will be the blueprint upon which all her future relationships will be drawn.

A girl's first perception of the opposite sex comes from her experience with her father. From this all-important relationship she develops her expectations of how a male should behave since her father becomes her unconscious model for all future romantic encounters. A girl's father provides her with her first love relationship with a man, and it is vital that she feel her father's unconditional acceptance. If her father is emotionally abusive, she will in turn expect other important men in her life to be the same.

To develop self-assurance a daughter needs to feel that her father accepts her and sees her as an attractive person both outside and inside. This provides the basis for her confidence as a woman and allows her to realize she is worthwhile and that, in future relationships with men, she should be respected. When a father gives his daughter the feeling that she is unattractive, either because he ignores her, is critical of her, or because he abandons her, he is paving the way for her to gravitate toward masochistic relationships where she will be treated poorly and without respect.

Emotionally Abusive Siblings

A woman's relationship with her siblings can be either a very positive or an extremely negative influence on her life. Unfortunately, all too often, a woman's sibling may be her first emotional abuser. So-called sibling rivalry that begins in childhood often continues well into adulthood. While it is natural for siblings to compare themselves with one another and to feel competitive, sometimes what passes for sibling rivalry is actually emotional abuse. Such a situation existed between Fran and her younger sister, Barbara.

Fran had always been jealous of Barbara. Barbara was more outgoing and more popular, and unlike Fran, she didn't have a weight problem. Life seemed to be so much easier for Barbara. She always had boyfriends, seemed to sail through school, and landed a great job right out of college. Fran, on the other hand, was a wallflower, had to work hard just to pass her classes, and later drifted aimlessly from one job to another.

The final blow to Fran was when Barbara, happily married for two years, had a beautiful baby daughter. Fran loved children and wanted a family more than anything, but the men she attracted always seemed to be losers.

Barbara was very aware that she had been the fortunate one in the family, and she felt bad for Fran because she knew she wasn't happy. She tried to make it up to Fran by trying to be a really loving sister, and she included Fran in her life as much as possible. But it never seemed to be enough—Fran always had a complaint about not being invited to Barbara's house enough, or about not getting to see the baby as often as she wanted.

Fran didn't even attempt to hide the fact that she was desperately jealous of Barbara. She constantly made remarks about how good Barbara had it, and she insinuated that she didn't deserve what she had. Whenever Barbara invited Fran to any of her social gatherings, Fran would always make a point of demeaning Barbara in front of her guests, saying such things as "I guess when you're born with a silver spoon in your mouth, you think you deserve the best of everything," or "Some of us have had to *work* for what we have, while others have just had it handed to them."

Barbara was terribly hurt by these remarks, because she really loved her sister and even admired her. But as time went on and Fran became more frustrated with her own life, her remarks became more and more cruel. Barbara tried reasoning with Fran, but it was to no avail. She didn't want to stop inviting Fran to her home, because she knew it would hurt her sister a lot. She just didn't know what to do.

She finally realized that unless the two of them got help, they would have to stop seeing each other. She asked Fran to go into therapy with her. To her surprise, Fran agreed, and the sisters were able to work things out.

Emotionally Abusive Friends

Since we rely on our friends for honest feedback, support, and companionship, they have a tremendous influence on us. If they disapprove of us, of our choices in partners, or of our job or career choices, they can influence our feelings about these things. Even if we disagree with a friend's opinion, we usually assume that she has our best interests at heart. But what if she doesn't? What if she is operating out of envy or jealousy, or even out of a need to destroy us?

Dee's best friend, Lucy, was extremely jealous of her, but Dee didn't realize it. Because she felt so close to Lucy, she trusted her judgment and motivation. Unbeknownst to Dee, Lucy tried to undermine her at every turn. She talked Dee out of going to night school by telling her that it was stupid, since it would take her forever to get a college degree that way. In actuality, Lucy was envious of Dee's intellect and motivation. When Dee told Lucy she was thinking about asking for a raise, Lucy once again talked her out of it. After all, if Dee got a raise, she'd be making more than Lucy. And whenever Dee became attracted to a man, Lucy always found something wrong with him. She didn't want Dee to have a boyfriend if she didn't.

TAKING STEPS TOWARD RECOVERY

Because of the undermining nature of emotional abuse, because it tears down your self-esteem and causes you to doubt yourself and your perceptions, you will undoubtedly continue to question whether or not you are actually being emotionally abused. You may sometimes think that you are just feeling sorry for yourself, or that you are making a big deal out of nothing. Even if you are able to hold on to the fact that you are indeed being emotionally abused, you may still believe that you deserve to be treated in an abusive manner. Your abusive mate might tell you that he wouldn't get so angry with you if he didn't love you so much. Your abusive boss might apologize for yelling at you, but at the same time excuse his behavior by telling you that he wouldn't get so angry with you if you tried harder or listened to his instructions better. It is important for you to understand that an emotional abuser will always blame his victim for his abusiveness and will always have an excuse for his behavior.

If you are being emotionally abused by someone, or if you recognize that you have established a pattern of consistently

CHAPTER 2

Types of Emotionally Abused Women

While all emotionally abused women share many of the same characteristics, their personality traits can differ. Identifying which type of emotionally abused woman you are will help you in several ways. It will help you to recognize how and why you allow others to abuse you. It will also help you to understand why you have a tendency to choose a particular type of abusive person to get involved with, and will thus help you to avoid this type of person in the future. Last, but certainly not least, identifying the type of emotionally abused person you are will help you to focus on what you need to do to avoid future abuse. Even though you may find that you identify with more than one of the following categories of emotionally abused women, there is probably one you relate to most.

THE "SELFLESS" WOMAN

The selfless woman is one with a very shaky sense of identity. Because her mother was either too smothering and controlling and didn't allow her to separate from her, or because her mother was rejecting and abandoning and didn't provide adequate nurturing, the selfless woman did not develop a strong identity and sense of self.

In her book *Sweet Suffering: Woman As Victim*, Natalie Shainess recognizes that an overprotective mother can be extremely detrimental to her child.

"An overprotective mother binds her child to her by refusing to allow the child to move away from her. Unable to recognize the separateness of her daughter, unable to acknowledge the boundaries between them, such a mother refuses to let the child develop her own thoughts and perceptions. This symbiotic relationship breeds passivity and a sense of inadequacy in the child."

Some mothers, themselves deprived of necessary nurturing and care when they were children, are incapable of being what psychoanalyst D. W. Winnicott calls "good enough" mothers to their children. The good-enough mother is there for her child both physically and emotionally, providing continuity, responding readily to her child, and believing from the start that her baby exists in her own right. Without good-enough mothering, a child is deprived of the very foundation upon which it can build a self.

To overcome her indistinct and mostly negative self-image, the selfless woman may "take on" the personality, identity, or appearance of another person. She often suffers from chronic feelings of emptiness, depression, and helplessness. A selfless woman usually has an extraordinary sensitivity to real or imagined rejection, and while she can be clingy and possessive at times, she can also be very rejecting of others. This is because she both craves and fears intimacy. She fears both being abandoned and being smothered—the latter coming from her fear of losing what little self she has. Needless to say, this makes it difficult for her to maintain stable relationships, since she frequently gives mixed messages ("Come here—go away").

Romantic attachments for the selfless woman are highly charged, filled with turbulence and rage, and they are usually short-lived. Although she feels continually victimized by others, this woman continues to desperately seek out new relationships, because for her being alone feels more intolerable than mistreatment.

Because of her deep self-loathing, the selfless woman distrusts others' expressions of caring. She often pursues those who are inaccessible and runs away if her overtures are accepted.

She seldom learns from past mistakes. Since she doesn't often observe patterns in her own behavior, she tends to repeat destructive relationships. For example, a selfless woman will often return to an abusive ex-husband, who will proceed to abuse her again.

No matter what others do to hurt or betray her, she keeps forgiving them, believing that they have finally learned their lesson and are going to change. She may decide never to see an abusive person again after he has finally done something so horrible to her that even she has to admit it is unacceptable. But before long, she has allowed herself to be charmed back into believing in the person again. She has convinced herself that this time he is truly sorry, that he has changed.

Cheryl's description of herself is a classic portrait of the selfless woman:

> I don't know who I am. I'm like a chameleon—I change according to who I'm around. When I'm around my friend Marsha, I become very quiet like her. But when I'm around Penny I laugh and joke a lot, because she's so outgoing. I even take on my friends' gestures and facial expressions.
>
> I do the same thing when I'm involved with a man. I become whatever the man I'm involved with wants me to be. If he wants me to be a sex kitten, that's who I am. If he wants a drinking buddy, that's me. If he wants someone to control, I let him control me. Then, when the relationship is over, I don't even have myself to come back to.
>
> I'm always trying to figure out what other people want from me in order to be accepted by them. I am seldom myself, because I assume others wouldn't like me if I were. Sometimes I wish I could just be totally alone and not have to bother with other people, but I'm afraid to be alone.

The following questions may further help you decide if you are a selfless woman:

☐ Do you tend to blame yourself when things go wrong?

☐ If you make a mistake, do you see yourself as all bad?

☐ Do you try to anticipate what others want or how they want you to act?

☐ Do you placate others, or try to "buy" them, in an attempt to keep harm at bay?

☐ Do you have a difficult time with change?

☐ Does taking risks make you feel frightened or apprehensive?

☐ Do you have a history of alcohol or drug abuse, eating disorders, sexual promiscuity, compulsive gambling or shopping, shoplifting, self-mutilation, or suicide attempts?

☐ Do you often have violent outbursts of rage?

THE PLEASER

Pleasers are always trying to keep everyone happy. Their motto is "Peace at any price," and the price they pay is often damage to their self-esteem. They want to keep everything smooth and on an even keel, and they often sacrifice their own happiness in the process.

These women learned to be pleasers when they were little girls, often because their mothers modeled this behavior. Brought up in an atmosphere in which they were made to feel inferior and unworthy simply because they were female, they now have a strong need to be "good girls" so that men will approve of them. They are obedient to authority figures—especially men—and they basically believe that most people are better than they are.

In addition, children who are deprived often feel so insignificant and worthless that they feel they need to justify their existence by becoming a source of help to their parents. Such children begin a lifelong pattern of pleasing others as a way of proving that they are worth keeping around.

Many pleasers were raised by parents who expected perfection from them and who put a lot of pressure on them to perform. Because of this, as adults they seldom feel they are worth much or that they are really appreciated, valued, or loved for themselves. Instead, they believe they have to earn others' acceptance and love. They believe that they count only when they are making others happy or doing everything perfectly. Pleasers want everyone to like them and to approve of what they do.

Kay is a typical pleaser. Her entire life is centered around her husband and her two children. Raised in a very traditional family where she was taught that a woman's purpose was to please her husband, her only ambition as a young girl was to become a wife and mother. She was married at nineteen, and she had had both of her children by the time she was twenty-one. Although she says her greatest pleasure is in pleasing her family, she is also becoming more and more dissatisfied with her life. Kay told me,

> I do everything to please my husband and children. The problem is that no matter what I do, they never seem satisfied. I give and give, but it is never enough. I get tired of it sometimes, but mostly I feel so satisfied when I know I've pleased them that it's all worth it.

For Kay, pleasing her husband includes having sex with him whenever he wants it, even though she seldom enjoys it.

> He really isn't a good lover. He's just concerned with satisfying himself. I resent this sometimes, and I have tried talking to him about what I need, but he just doesn't seem to listen. So I have sex just to please him, so he'll be happy.

While Kay makes her husband and family her top priority, her husband neglects her severely.

> He isn't an affectionate man. In fact, he doesn't really ever touch me unless he wants sex. He never has a kind word to say to me, although I know he loves me. I just wish he would tell me once in a while that I have done something that pleased him, or that he appreciates all I do for him.

While the pleaser may get depressed, frustrated, or angry at times because of the way she is treated, she continues to put up with the most abusive treatment. She often rationalizes that things could be worse. She makes excuses for her abusers' scorn, bad tempers, or lack of consideration, or else she convinces herself that she can change them.

Even if she knows that an abuser is wrong, she will take the blame and apologize, because this will at least keep the peace. In order to be accepted or loved she will even apologize for perfectly appropriate behavior on her part.

You may be a pleaser if you answer yes to many of the following questions:

☐ Do you feel that you count only when you are taking care of others?

☐ Do you feel that you can't do most things right?

☐ Are you always saying, "I should have . . . " or "I ought to . . . "?

☐ Do you have a difficult time saying no?

☐ Do your husband and children always know how to make you feel guilty?

☐ Do you often pretend to be enjoying yourself when you're not?

☐ Do you often "fake it," telling others that you like or approve of what they are doing or saying when you don't?

☐ Are you nice to other people because you hope they'll be nice to you in return?

THE SINNER

The sinner has many of the same qualities as the pleaser. However, the sinner also suffers from intense feelings of guilt and shame, which play an important role in her motivation to please.

The sinner always feels responsible, always believes that "it's my fault." Often, this tendency to blame herself comes from her having been severely criticized as a child. Constantly apologizing, she obsesses about "if only"—if only she had done something differently, if only she'd said the right thing. . . .

Frequently, sinners were victims of either overt or emotional sexual abuse as children. Made to feel dirty, shameful, and bad, as adults they carry their guilt and shame around as though these were scarlet letters. Because she feels guilty about real or imagined past mistakes, the sinner is often plagued with the belief that she doesn't really deserve to be treated well, respected, or loved, and that she needs to suffer in order to atone for her sins.

Sinners may feel guilty, worthless, and bad because as

children they were given the message that there was something inherently wrong with them. In addition, parents who are rigidly religious often give their children heavy doses of guilt and make them believe they are sinners for not always obeying and honoring their parents. Sinners also believe that bad things only happen to bad people. When something bad does happen to them, they believe that they must have deserved it or it wouldn't have happened.

Katie was raised by a hypercritical mother who made her feel as though she were to blame for all of her mother's problems. Born out of wedlock, Katie always knew she wasn't wanted, and she felt that if it weren't for her birth, her mother would have not had to marry her abusive, alcoholic father.

> Nothing I ever did was right. I was constantly ridiculed for my behavior and lectured to about what a bad child I was. My mother seemed to assume that I should already know the proper way to conduct myself at all times, and she was very impatient with me for making even the slightest mistake. Whenever I did something wrong, she assumed it was intentional and accused me of deliberately trying to make her miserable. I grew up with a terrible case of guilt, and this carried over into my relationship with my husband—who, by the way, is just like my mother. He blamed me for everything, and because I felt guilty for just *breathing,* I always took the blame.

Sinners tend to

- ☐ get involved with those who are cruel, uncaring, and abusive
- ☐ suffer intense feelings of self-loathing
- ☐ feel they must pay for their past sins
- ☐ be unable to forgive themselves for past mistakes
- ☐ be self-denigrating and self-critical
- ☐ always blame themselves for whatever goes wrong

Trudy is a typical sinner. This is how she describes her relationship with her husband, who is extremely emotionally abusive:

I try so hard to be patient with my husband, because I know he doesn't feel well sometimes. He has ulcers, and when they act up he's a real bear. I know I should be more understanding, but honestly, sometimes it gets hard. He's so demanding and so critical of me. Sometimes I get very angry with him, and I know I shouldn't because he can't help it. I probably deserve a lot of his criticism because I don't do the things for him I used to do, but I am so tired of his complaining that I resent helping him out.

I don't like the way I feel, but I don't know what to do to change. I pray to God to help me be more understanding and to be a better wife, and I have even gone to my minister for counseling a few times. He tells me to be more patient and to work on forgiving my husband, and I know he is right. I hold grudges against my husband, and I'm not forgiving. I just keep hearing the terrible things he has said about me over and over in my head. Sometimes I think I'm crazy, or that I *want* to keep remembering what he's said to me. I'm not a very forgiving person, you know.

Because Trudy feels so bad about herself, she is unable to recognize just how inappropriate her husband's behavior is and how much this abusive behavior is damaging her. Instead, she takes total responsibility for the relationship, and she constantly chastises herself for being angry even though her anger is justifiable.

THE CODEPENDENT

There are many definitions of codependency, and much of the behavior we have discussed in the above categories can be construed as codependent behavior. But the type of emotionally abused woman I am describing in this category is the type defined by Melody Beattie, author of *Codependent No More* and *Beyond Codependency,* as "one who has let another person's behavior affect him or her, and who is obsessed with controlling that person's behavior." A codependent has a pattern of getting involved with people whom she tries to rescue or take care of, and she lives her life for others. She anticipates other people's needs, and she then wonders why they don't do the same for her.

In addition, she often finds herself doing more than her fair share of the work and doing things for others that they are capable of doing for themselves. Then, when others do not do what she wants, she feels victimized, angry, unappreciated, and used.

Children brought up in homes where one or both parents are addicted to alcohol, drugs, food, gambling, shopping, and so on can become codependent. Growing up in a dysfunctional or addictive family causes a child to feel out of control. Many children try to gain a sense of control by becoming "pseudo-adults," and attempting to control their behavior.

Codependent women have very low self-esteem and often feel that their lives aren't worth living. Only when they are giving to others do they feel worthwhile, since they get artificial feelings of self-worth from helping others. These rescuers often enjoy the appearance of being a "savior." Because they don't feel worthy of having friendship or love just because of who they are, they encourage others to be dependent on their ability and willingness to rescue. They constantly try to prove they are good enough for other people, but they settle for being needed.

Codependents don't feel happy or content with themselves, so they look outside themselves for happiness. They latch on to whomever or whatever they think can provide happiness. In their desperate search for love and approval they often seek love from people who are incapable of loving. They worry that people will leave them, and they feel terribly threatened by the loss of anyone or anything they think can provide them with happiness.

Codependent women have a difficult time asserting their own needs, wants, and rights and expressing their emotions openly, honestly, and appropriately, especially the emotions of anger and hurt. They repress their own anger, and they are afraid of other people's anger.

They complain, blame, and try to control, yet they continue to allow others to hurt them. In actuality, codependents are a lot more comfortable in complaining and in feeling resentful and bitter than in acknowledging how very hurt and angry they are. They push their thoughts and feelings out of their awareness by focusing all of their awareness and energy on other people. They stay busy so they won't have to think about things and face reality. They ignore problems and pretend they aren't happening, and they pretend that circumstances are not as bad as they really are. They believe the lies of others, even when others have been known to lie to them before.

The irony is that as much as a codependent feels responsible for others and takes care of others, she believes deep down that other people are somehow responsible for her. She blames others for her unhappiness and her problems, and she feels that if it weren't for the problem people in her life, she would be happy.

Another irony is that while she feels controlled by people and events, she is herself overly controlling. She is afraid of allowing other people to be who they are and of allowing events to happen naturally. An expert in knowing best how things should turn out and how people should behave, the codependent woman tries to control others through coercion, threats, advice-giving, helplessness, guilt, manipulation, or domination. Last but not least, she is afraid to let herself be who she really is, and she thus often appears rigid and controlled.

Stacey is a codependent. She has been married to an alcoholic for fifteen years, and during this time she has focused a great deal of her time and energy on trying to make her husband stop drinking:

> I feel so stuck. I've tried everything to get Josh to stop drinking, but nothing has worked. I know I should probably leave him, but I'm afraid of what he'd do if I weren't around. I think he'd just drink himself to death. I feel so angry with him for not sobering up. He keeps losing jobs, and we keep getting further and further into debt. It could have been so different if he weren't a drunk. We'd have a nicer house, and the kids could go to college. Now we can barely make ends meet, and it's all because of Josh's drinking.

If you feel you are a codependent person, the following questions, adapted from Melody Beattie's *Codependent No More,* will help you to decide:

- ☐ Do you feel responsible for other people—for their feelings, thoughts, actions, choices, wants, needs, well-being, and destiny?

☐ Do you feel compelled to help people solve their problems by offering unsolicited advice, by giving a rapid-fire series of suggestions, or by trying to take care of their feelings?

☐ Do you find it easier to feel and express anger about injustices done to others than about injustices done to you?

☐ Do you feel safest and most comfortable when you are giving to others?

☐ Do you feel insecure and guilty when someone gives to you?

☐ Do you feel empty, bored, and worthless if you don't have someone else to take care of, a problem to solve, or a crisis to deal with?

☐ Do you often try to catch others in acts of misbehavior?

☐ Are you often unable to stop talking, thinking, and worrying about other people and their problems?

☐ Do you lose interest in your own life when you are in love?

☐ Do you worry that other people will leave you?

☐ Do you stay in relationships that don't work and tolerate abuse in order to keep people loving you?

☐ Do you leave bad relationships only to form new ones that don't work, either?

If you answered yes to more than half of these questions, you are probably codependent.

THE DRAMA JUNKIE

Many codependents may also be drama junkies, but not all drama junkies are codependents. Drama junkies were usually raised in dysfunctional, highly chaotic homes where there was alcohol or drug abuse, frequent fighting between the parents, physical abuse, or other forms of frequent disruption or upset. Also sometimes referred to as "adrenaline junkies," drama junkies have become accustomed to a tremendous amount of change, violence, and crisis and emergency situations. Often depressed and anxious when life is stable or uneventful, these women feel truly alive only after surviving a threatening or highly charged experience.

Heidi described what it's like to be a drama junkie:

> As a kid, I got lots of strokes for taking care of my younger brothers while my mother worked or went to the bars, and for holding my own with my alcoholic father and still being able to keep up my grades at school. People who knew my situation at home couldn't believe I could handle it all, and they gave me a lot of credit for being able to do it so well. Even after I left home I noticed that I always did well in a crisis, and I loved the recognition I got for taking care of things with such a cool head.
>
> Now, though, I notice that I don't really feel alive unless I am under pressure or handling some kind of crisis. I think I even sometimes create crises so I can get the good feeling of knowing I can handle it.

Although a chaotic home environment is usually the primary cause of this problem, the opposite is also sometimes true. For example, a child who is isolated and thus prevented from making appropriate social contacts with others, or who is deprived of adequate stimulation, can become a drama junkie. This was Rebecca's experience:

> I couldn't wait until I left my parents' house and got out in the real world. I moved to the city right away, and I went crazy with my newfound freedom. I went out with lots of guys, especially ones who could take me places and show me things. I got into drugs and ended up hanging around with a lot of guys who were very abusive to me, but it all seemed so exciting after the kind of childhood I had had.
>
> Now, even though I'm off drugs, I'm still attracted to abusive guys. And I find I still tend to stir things up when it gets too quiet. I always get into some kind of trouble—if it's not getting a speeding ticket, it's having a fight with someone.

Women who are drama junkies are not interested in meeting healthy, normal men who will treat them with love and respect. These men would, they feel, be too boring. Instead, drama junkies prefer the excitement of someone who is distant and hard to reach, someone they can't be too sure of, even someone who is abusive. Kim, who had been a client of mine for quite some time, was finally able to see that she had this tendency:

> I guess the sicker the guy is or the more unavailable he is, the more attractive he is to me. I like the challenge, the "hard cases," the guys who run away or push me away. The more they reject me, the more I want them. When a guy is nice to me, he actually turns me off. I absolutely can't *stand* a guy who is really sweet—in fact, that kind of guy is repulsive to me.

If you find yourself answering yes to many of the following questions, you may be a drama junkie:

1. Are you almost always angry with at least one person in your life?
2. Do you frequently find yourself in heated arguments with lovers, friends, coworkers, or family members?
3. Are your reunions after fights or separations from your lover intensely erotic?
4. Is there almost always some kind of a crisis occurring in your life?
5. Do you find yourself needing to "stir things up" when things get too calm?
6. Do you get bored easily?
7. Do you tend to be unhappy with routine and instead prefer a lifestyle that involves continual change?
8. Do you ever wonder whether anyone or anything will ever really make you happy?
9. Do you often have fantasies that are filled with violence or illicit sex?
10. Do you tend to become attracted to and get involved with men who are unavailable, who aren't interested in you, who are abusive, or who have problems?

THE VICTIM OR MARTYR

As mentioned in chapter 1, women are frequently the victims of inequality, prejudice, and misogynism in our society. And socialization often supports this role. While boys are encouraged to fight back when others violate them, girls are encouraged to do nothing. The helplessness a girl may have learned in childhood often carries over into adulthood, so that passivity may seem to be the only way to handle problems. In addition, if a girl was raised in a home where she saw her mother being beaten or otherwise victimized by her husband or boyfriend, she may also conclude that being a woman is synonymous with being a victim.

Because of these experiences, many women have what is frequently called a victim mentality. In fact, all of the types of emotionally abused women mentioned above have this characteristic in common. However, some women can be characterized almost exclusively by a victim mentality. Some believe that life is one bad thing after another, and that there is nothing they can do to control their lives in any way. Others need continuing adversity in order to keep proving their worth and strengths. These women see life as a series of ordeals to survive and obstacles to overcome. Some actually have an investment in seeing themselves as a great or constant sufferer—in other words, a martyr. A martyr is one who voluntarily sacrifices her own health, happiness, or well-being for others.

The most common cause of a victim mentality is having had one parent who was hypercritical, overcontrolling, domineering, or raging and another who was passive, inadequate, or codependent. This teaches the child that in any given situation, there is always a victim and a victimizer.

When Tanya first came to see me, she described her problems this way:

> I have lived out my life as a victim. If someone else has any authority over me or seems stronger or better than me in any way, I give myself over to them. I am threatened by anyone who is strong-willed or who has any power. I can't speak up for myself, no matter how much someone takes advantage of me. I allow everyone to abuse me in some

way. My boss takes advantage of me, my friends use me, and my boyfriends usually end up walking all over me. I'm a real doormat.

As it turned out, Tanya had always had the fantasy that someone stronger than she was could take care of her. The price she paid was that she continually became involved with people who bossed her around and tried to control her.

The following questions will help you to determine whether you are a victim. If you answer yes to half of these questions or more, you are suffering from a victim mentality.

☐ Do you feel you have to "walk on eggshells" to keep others from getting angry?

☐ Are you fearful of confrontations?

☐ Do you overapologize? Are you too polite? Do you find yourself always saying, "I'm sorry"—sorry for being late, sorry for interrupting, sorry for talking too long?

☐ Do you feel overpowered by your husband, boyfriend, parents, or boss?

☐ Do you feel that you can't do anything right?

☐ Do you often feel like running away or not dealing with things?

☐ Do you often feel as though you are not running your own life?

☐ Do you have a hard time saying no?

☐ When you do stand up for your rights, do you feel frightened or embarrassed?

☐ Do you feel you have few options or choices for improving your life?

☐ Do you often feel that people don't appreciate you?

☐ Do you always assume the worst?

☐ When you are presented with a problem, do you usually become overwhelmed with doubts and fears and assume you will not be able to cope with the situation?

☐ Do you feel helpless and immobilized in a crisis?

☐ Do you let situations deteriorate into catastrophes or exaggerate them into appearing so?

In this chapter you were introduced to yourself. In the next chapter you will be introduced to the emotional abuser—the type of person who is bent on undermining, confusing, or even destroying another person. By the end of that chapter you will have learned how to recognize various types of abusers, their motivations, and the ways in which they operate. You'll meet emotionally abusive lovers, bosses, coworkers, siblings, and friends—people who may seem all to familiar to you—and you'll learn about the all-too-lethal attraction between particular types of abused women and abusers.

The Many Faces
of the Emotional Abuser

It is vital for you to understand the emotional abuser, not for the purpose of changing him or her, but to help you come to the realization of how destructive this person is and begin to put the responsibility for the abuse where it belongs.

The emotionally abusive person has an agenda, and that agenda is to be in control. In his attempt to be in control he will dominate, suppress, tyrannize, persecute, and attempt to conquer anyone he relates to on a consistent basis. Among his repertoire of control tactics are insults, denigrating comments, derogatory words, threats, and constant criticism, along with an extensive array of other intimidating behavior designed to make others feel inadequate and helpless. His most obvious tactics involve yelling, threatening, temper tantrums, name calling, and constant criticism. Direct and out in the open, these attacks have an aggressive, assaultive quality about them. But he also has an array of less obvious tactics that are insidious and covert, such as implied threats, unrelenting criticism in the guise of teaching or guiding you, gaslighting, denial, rewriting history, and shifting the blame.

An emotional abuser:

- ☐ Needs to be in control of the situation and the relationship; feels out of control of himself, so has to control the environment and other people.

- ☐ Needs to dominate other people in order to feel powerful and important.

- [ ] Has low self-esteem and is threatened by others' achievements and accomplishments.

- [ ] Feels insecure and inadequate. Has to constantly prove himself or tear others down in order to make himself look good.

- [ ] Blames others for his own shortcomings and for his problems.

- [ ] Feels his needs are more important than others' needs.

- [ ] Is insensitive, unable to see another person's point of view and to empathize with another's feelings.

- [ ] Feels he is always right.

- [ ] Is impatient, irritable, and short-tempered.

- [ ] Has unrealistic, unreasonable expectations of others.

- [ ] Is a perfectionist.

- [ ] Can be extremely distant, cold, and unresponsive, especially when you are not in his "good graces" or when he desires to punish or control you.

- [ ] Is unforgiving and holds grudges.

- [ ] Can be very mercurial, shifting from one extreme mood to another.

- [ ] Is untrusting, suspicious, and jealous.

- [ ] Is angry, resentful, tense, and frustrated.

TRUE TO TYPE: SPECIFIC M.O.'S OF EMOTIONAL ABUSERS

In addition to sharing many of the general traits just listed, some emotional abusers can also be characterized (and thus further categorized) by their intentions or motivations and by their specific methods of being emotionally abusive. The following sections describe the most common types of emotional abusers (there are, of course, some abusers you have met who are not listed here). Many of the different types can overlap, and you may find that two or three categories taken together may describe your abuser.

The Possessor

Possessors feel extremely insecure and inadequate, and so are desperately afraid of loss. They want to own, or possess, others as a way of guaranteeing that they will never be left or abandoned. Their message is: "Above all, always be available to me."

A husband or lover who is a possessor will be very demanding of your time, energy, and affection. He is never satisfied, and his needs seem endless. He wants to spend every waking hour with you, he can't get enough of you sexually, and he constantly wants you to do things for him to show him that you love him. If you try to take time for yourself, he becomes even more demanding, insisting that you don't really love him—otherwise, you would want to be with him as much as he wants to be with you. A possessive husband or boyfriend can also be extremely jealous, assuming that you are always flirting with other men or suspecting you of having affairs.

The danger in this situation is that in constantly trying to please this person but never succeeding, you can lose yourself.

VICTOR: ABUSIVE EXPECTATIONS, DOMINATION   During Denise's five-year marriage to Victor, he continually accused her of being unfaithful. If he answered the phone and the caller hung up, Victor assumed it was a man calling for Denise. He wanted to know where she was at all times, and he called her at work five or six times a day to make sure she was there. If she wasn't at her desk he would interrogate whoever answered her phone to find out where she was, when she had left, and even who she was with. Because Victor was so jealous and insecure, Denise made a point of coming directly home from work each day. If she was even a few minutes late he would accuse her of having been with another man.

When Denise became pregnant, Victor insisted that the baby was not his, although he had no rational reason for this belief. No matter how much Denise tried to reassure him, he wouldn't change his mind. He became obsessed with catching her with her secret lover, and he even went so far as to have the telephone bugged so he could monitor her calls. He opened her mail, searched her dresser drawers, and inspected the inside of her car every time she had been out.

Each time Denise discovered that Victor had been spying on her she became more and more upset. She was embarrassed by Victor's actions, and her work had begun to suffer. She became increasingly nervous, constantly anticipating Victor's next accusation. She tried even harder to convince him that she loved him, feeling that perhaps she wasn't giving him enough of her time and attention. But this only caused him to doubt her more, suspecting that she was "buttering him up" so he'd stop checking on her so much.

In desperation, Denise begged Victor to get counseling, but he refused, saying that he wasn't the one with the problem. Finally, as a last resort, she decided to seek counseling to learn to cope with his jealousy. This was the turning point in her life, since through counseling she became aware that she had been taking responsibility for Victor's problems instead of recognizing that she was being victimized by them.

Husbands and lovers aren't the only possessors. Bosses can also be very possessive, demanding too much of their employee's time and attention. In addition, some parents refuse to let their children grow up and possessively hang on to them even when they are grown. They demand that their adult children visit them more often, telephone more frequently, and take responsibility for running their errands and doing their chores. Possessive parents may be critical of any man their daughter dates, because they do not want her to get married; they want to keep her all to themselves.

Even a friend can be possessive, wanting you to have no other friends or wanting to make sure that she is your best friend. Some friends may be critical of all the men you date, for fear of losing you if you get too serious with a man.

The Napoleon

Napoleons tear others down to make themselves look good. Secretly feeling that they are "less than" others, either because they have a real or an imagined deficit or handicap, they, like the famed Napoleon, overcompensate for their deficiency by becoming bullies and making fun of others.

Men who are insecure about their size, masculinity, or lack of success will often become involved with women they can ridicule and put down as a way of making themselves feel better. Friends, siblings, and coworkers who are insecure or jealous of our success will sometimes put us down as a way of building themselves up.

RICK: CONSTANT CRITICISM, CHARACTER ASSASSINATION   By the time Sally finally came into therapy, she had been so severely damaged by her boyfriend, Rick, that she could hardly hold a job. When Sally first met Rick she was an attractive, extremely bright young woman with a good job, a beautiful apartment, an active social life, and many close friends. But during her four-year relationship with Rick, her self-esteem had been torn down to the point at which her job was in jeopardy, she had lost nearly all her friends, and she had gained forty pounds.

Rick had set out to make Sally believe she was so stupid, ugly, and unlovable that she was lucky to have him because no one else would want her. He told her that she wasn't as pretty as the other girls he had dated, that she wasn't good in bed, and that his friends didn't think she was good enough for him. He constantly told her that he didn't know how she had gotten such a well-paying job. He also told her that her girlfriends were always coming on to him behind her back.

It wasn't until Sally joined Overeaters Anonymous (OA), a Twelve-Step program for compulsive overeaters, that she began to realize that a great deal of her weight problem was due to Rick's constant criticism. When she talked about her relationship with Rick at OA meetings, she was surprised when others told her that Rick sounded hypercritical, that the relationship sounded destructive, and that she was blaming herself too much for the problems in the relationship. Like many emotionally abused women, Sally needed support and feedback from others to help her break away from the clutches of an emotionally abusive man. With only Rick as a point of reference, she would have continued to believe his criticism, and over time she would have lost all confidence and sense of self-worth.

The Bulldozers

These people mow over everyone in their path, tearing others down in order to get their own needs met. They are insensitive to the needs of others, making only their needs important.

Women usually encounter this type of personality in business, where the bulldozer may be a boss or coworker. These people are often power hungry and will do just about anything to get ahead. While they sometimes camouflage their true natures under the guise of offering guidance and assistance, they are always out for number one. Their goals are all that are important to them—not people.

MARCUS: DOMINATION, CONSTANT CRITICISM Sometimes emotional abuse is couched as "helping out" or as something that is necessary to "get the job done." Marcus was the owner of a small, independent record company. A shrewd businessman, he was fairly successful and had produced a number of hit albums. Although he was known for giving new recording artists a break, none of them stayed with him after their first album.

Sabrina was just such an artist. At her first meeting with Marcus she found him to be stern and extremely businesslike, but straightforward and encouraging. Although he expressed a few concerns about her physical appearance, he offered her a contract right away. Sabrina was very grateful for Marcus's faith in her and his willingness to take a chance on an unknown.

Once the two started working together, however, Marcus slowly began to tear away at Sabrina's self-esteem. Under the guise of "helping her out," he suggested to her that in order to sell records she needed to lose weight and eliminate a slight lisp. These were things that Sabrina had felt self-conscious about for a long time, so she took Marcus's suggestions to heart and started a diet, hired a personal trainer, and began working with a speech therapist.

Had Sabrina then been allowed to progress at her own speed, Marcus's suggestions that she work on these problems would not necessarily have been abusive. But he kept a close watch on her progress, constantly reminding her that she had to eliminate these problems in order to sell records. This put a tremendous amount of pressure on Sabrina—so much, in fact, that the pressure ended up sabotaging her chance for success. With so much focus placed on how she looked and how she sounded when she talked, Sabrina began to lose what was truly the most important thing for her career—her songs, and how she sounded when she sang.

Slowly, Sabrina began to lose confidence in her singing and in her song-writing ability. Again, Marcus was instrumental in her loss of belief in herself. Whenever Sabrina wrote a good song, he would focus on the song's weaknesses and call someone in to help her with it. After the song had been changed slightly, he would go on and on about how much better it was, saying, "*We've* written a good song." After hearing her sing he would always say something like, "You're getting there," or "Maybe you should stick with slow songs." Even when Sabrina had felt like she had sounded her best she wouldn't get a compliment from Marcus.

Finally, Sabrina's album was completed, and she was scheduled for some guest appearances on television. After her first appearance, Marcus called her in to give her some "feedback." Instead of saying anything about her song or her singing, however, he reminded her that television makes everyone look heavier, and he said that because she hadn't yet lost enough weight she had looked fat on the show. He also told her that her lisp was still there and was very distracting. Sabrina became extremely anxious about making any more public appearances and eventually refused to do any more interviews, even though her album was selling very well.

Sabrina was so devastated by her experience with Marcus that she was unable to make another record for several years. It wasn't until she entered therapy that she became aware of how emotionally abusive Marcus had been to her and how much he had sabotaged her career. He had been so bent on her being "perfect" so that he would have a hit album that he had squashed her talent.

The Controllers

Some people have such a need to control that they deserve a special category all their own. These people can be possessors,

Napoleons, or bulldozers, but they also want to control just for the sake of controlling. Some are compulsive in their need to be organized, while others gain tremendous satisfaction from dominating others. Most control because they are afraid of being *out* of control, but some do so in order to feel powerful. It is very important to controllers that they get their way. If they don't, they may threaten, have "temper tantrums," pout, or withdraw in an icy silence. The controller *has* to win—in business, in sports, and even in love.

A controlling husband expects to have his will obeyed. After all, he feels, he is the head of the household—the boss. If you do not do what he wants, he will punish you. Some controllers punish by being physically or verbally abusive, while others do so by "teaching you a lesson" (staying out all night, leaving without saying where they are going, having affairs). Still others simply withdraw, refusing to talk to you and ignoring you or pouting.

A controlling husband tries to control not only your life, but your children's lives as well. These men are tyrants in their homes, forcing their children to follow unreasonable rules and submit to their will. If you try to reason with such a person, he just becomes more irate. There is no reasoning with a controlling person; he is out of control.

MR. EDWARDS: DOMINATION, VERBAL ABUSE   Judy's boss, Mr. Edwards, was a tyrant. Instead of asking her politely to do something, he ordered her to do it. He overloaded her with work and then complained when she couldn't get it all done. If he didn't like what she had done he would become verbally abusive, telling her she was stupid and incompetent.

Judy put up with this mistreatment because she was afraid she would not be able to get another job. She knew Mr. Edwards wouldn't give her a good recommendation, and she didn't have any previous experience to put on a job application. As a single mother with two small children and no child support, she desperately needed a job.

Eventually, Judy's health began to suffer as a result of the constant criticism and verbal abuse. She began to have migraine headaches several times a week, and she developed an ulcer. Her doctor told her that she was suffering from stress and put her on medical disability for two weeks. He also referred her to me for counseling.

It was clear to me that even though Judy had no prior work experience, she was unrealistic in her belief that no one else would hire her. The problem was not her lack of experience but her low self-esteem. As we worked together, it became painfully clear to Judy that the longer she worked for Mr. Edwards, the lower her self-esteem would become.

Judy's health improved radically while she was off work. After one week away from the job, she told me, "I didn't really believe that my symptoms could be caused by stress, but now I realize how much that job is taking out of me."

Judy agreed to fill out a few job applications during her two weeks away from work, even though she was certain it would do no good. Much to her surprise, she received a call from one of the companies she had applied to and was asked to come in for an interview (and later was offered the job). Even though she didn't yet know when she went back to work whether she had the new job, she said that she no longer felt so powerless: "No matter what happened with the job offer, I now knew that there was hope for me to get out."

The Sex Addict

This person pleads or demands that you have sex with him every day, or even several times a day. If you refuse him, he becomes irate, acts hurt, or withdraws. He may insist that he desires sex with you so much simply because he loves you and because you "turn him on." The truth, however, is that his strong sexual drive has little or nothing to do with his feelings for you and it may not even have anything to do with sex. For this type of emotional abuser, sex has become a way of pushing down feelings that are given no healthy outlet. The sex addict learned during childhood that sex could relieve tension. He may have learned this by masturbating when he felt upset, angry, and hurt, or he may have been introduced to sex very early on (perhaps by an adult). As an adult, the sex addict seeks sexual release whenever he is under pressure or unhappy. Since having sex provides him with only a temporary physiological release and does not solve any of his problems, his demand for sex is continual.

Some sex addicts also use sex as a way to temporarily feel better about themselves or to feel powerful. The need to feel powerful may have come from the person's having been sexually abused as a child.

Besides demanding frequent sex, the sex addict may also insist that sex always involve "kinky" acts (for example, bondage, flagellation, or humiliation). He may constantly look at porno magazines, watch X-rated movies, or urge that the two of you explore alternative lifestyles, such as nudist colonies, swingers clubs, "wife-swapping," and bisexuality.

The Antisocial Personality

Antisocial personalities do not live by the same set of rules and values that most people do. This type of emotional abuser has his own set of rules, created with only his own desires in mind, to justify his antisocial acts. Grossly selfish, impulsive, and callous, this person is likely to be involved with illegal acts, gambling, pornography, sexual abuse, violence, and alcohol or drug abuse. He tends either to blame others for his behavior or to offer rationalizations to justify even the cruelest actions. He is usually incapable of having significant loyalties to others. Almost without exception, these people were severely abused physically, emotionally, verbally, and perhaps also sexually as children.

Antisocial personalities attempt to control others through manipulation or aggression. Such a person will promise everything, but deliver nothing but more promises. He will lie without compunction, telling his mate that he has paid the bills when instead he has gambled the money away or spent it on another woman. If confronted, he will lash out at his mate and make her feel sorry that she doubted him. Since his tolerance for frustration is low, he is quick to anger and can be very explosive, thus discouraging any real confrontation.

LARRY: CONSTANT CHAOS   Joanna's boyfriend, Larry, was an antisocial personality. For five years, Joanna's life was plagued by his drug abuse, womanizing, lying, and stealing from her. By the time she entered therapy, she had finally broken the relationship off, but she had had to move three times in an attempt to hide from Larry. She no longer had friends, since they had all become so disgusted with her for staying with Larry so long and so tired of hearing her complaints about him that they had finally stopped seeing her. When she came to see me, her self-esteem was incredibly low. "I can't believe I put up with Larry all that time," she said. "I just can't believe I let him do some of the things he did. I must be either stupid or crazy."

In actuality, she was neither. Like a number of other women, Joanna was a victim of an antisocial personality. Larry could be very charming when he needed to talk his way out of a predicament caused by his infantile and destructive ways. Each time he was caught taking drugs, womanizing, lying, or stealing, he would beg Joanna to forgive him. He would cry and tell her he loved her more than he had ever loved anyone in his life, and he'd promise never to do it again. Joanna described the situation to me:

> I loved him so much that I wanted to believe him. I would feel sorry for him because he had so many problems, and I really thought he wanted to change. I begged him to get help, but he always made up some excuse—he didn't have the money, or he thought all therapists were crazy themselves. He did go to one Narcotics Anonymous meeting, but he never went back. He said he wasn't like those people, that they were all hard-core addicts and he couldn't relate to them.
>
> Finally, I went to some Al-Anon meetings, for people with loved ones who are alcoholics or drug addicts. I learned that Larry had a serious problem, and that he was probably going to have to hit bottom before he admitted he needed help. I also learned I was doing the same thing my mother had done with my alcoholic father: I was enabling Larry to continue his drug taking and his other antisocial behavior by nagging at him and by continually making excuses for his behavior. I realized that it would take a while for Larry to hit bottom, and that in the meantime I was going down with him. I didn't want to make the same mistake my mother made with my father. I wanted out while I was still young, so I left.

The Narcissist

Narcissism is characterized by a grandiose sense of self-importance; recurrent fantasies of unlimited success, power, brilliance, beauty or ideal love; a craving for constant attention and admiration; and feelings of rage, humiliation, or haughty indifference when criticized or defeated. In addition, narcissists have at least two of the following characteristics: a sense of entitlement (that is, they view themselves as desirable, talented, and special and thus entitled to special recognition and unconditional acceptance); exploitativeness (the tendency to take advantage of others and to disregard their rights); oscillation between extreme overidealization and devaluation of others; and lack of empathy (meaning not just an inability to recognize how others feel but often also the inability to recognize that others have feelings at all).

Even though narcissists are often arrogant and vain and seem to feel superior to others, they in fact have very low self-esteem. They find it hard to accept constructive feedback of any kind or to go beyond superficial relationships.

RAOUL: GASLIGHTING, ABUSIVE EXPECTATIONS   Raoul was a ladies' man. He was handsome, charming, and fun to be with; consequently, women were consistently attracted to him. This was a continual problem for Tiffany, who had been going with Raoul for eight months. She was constantly being hurt by Raoul's tendency to flirt openly with other women and his insistence that he had the right to do so. Every time they would get into an argument over his flirting, Raoul would become irate with Tiffany and yell things at her like: "I can't help it if I am a great-looking guy and women find me attractive! You should feel proud that other women want your boyfriend," or "Hey, there's nothing wrong with looking, I'm not dead, you know. Maybe if you exercised a little more I wouldn't be so tempted to look around."

Tiffany would always become confused with Raoul's logic. She'd think to herself, "Well, he's right, he can't help it if he's good-looking and I should feel proud of him. And I should exercise more. After all, there are a lot of beautiful women out there and I could lose Raoul if I don't keep up my shape."

But the truth of the matter was that Raoul needed the admiration of other women to boost his sagging ego. And he was being totally insensitive to Tiffany's feelings by not understanding that his behavior was being hurtful to her. He was deliberately keeping her off-balance with his peculiar form of logic so that he could hold on to her and still have the freedom to see whomever he wanted.

The Misogynist

As noted earlier in the book, there are both male and female misogynists. A male misogynist has a lack of respect for women that permeates his every interaction with them, whether at work or at home. He devalues women by belittling them or making fun of them, by using them or mistreating them sexually, by seeing them as merely sex objects, or by becoming physically violent toward them.

A female misogynist is prejudiced against other women or has a deep distrust and dislike for them. Often, female misogynists were raised to believe that females are inferior to males. The female misogynist sees other women as enemies rather than allies, as her competition for the attention of males or for positions at work. She will back-stab, gossip about, or openly criticize any woman who gets in her way.

IRENE: ABUSIVE EXPECTATIONS Eleanor was emotionally abused by a misogynistic female boss. For six years, Eleanor had worked for a famous toy manufacturer, with the responsibility of coming up with new ideas for toys. She liked her job and was good at it. Things became difficult for her, however, when her old boss left and a new boss was hired. Almost immediately, the new boss, Irene, started treating Eleanor differently from the other workers under her supervision, all of whom were men.

Irene seemed suspicious and distrustful of Eleanor. Shortly after arriving, she called Eleanor into her office and lectured her about the importance of being on time, even though Eleanor had always been prompt. She also told Eleanor that she wouldn't be able to leave early to pick up her children, nor should she expect time off because of her children's illnesses or medical appointments—requests that Eleanor had never made. Not only did Irene make no such demands of the men in her department, but she openly joked with them about the long lunch hours they often took.

Irene also made it clear that she didn't trust Eleanor's ability to be innovative or creative, nor did she trust her honesty. Whenever Eleanor proposed a new design for a toy, Irene questioned her about where she had gotten the idea. On top of all this, she never liked any of Eleanor's ideas, even though her coworkers did.

After several of Eleanor's coworkers let her know they had noticed the unfair treatment and offered to back her up, she finally got the courage to make a formal complaint to her boss's superior. She knew she was taking a big chance, but her coworkers reassured her that she was a valuable employee and that she deserved to be heard. Fortunately, the superior valued Eleanor's work enough to step in and speak to Irene. Things seemed to change considerably after this. Eleanor was treated fairly and equally from that time on. Although Irene still made it clear that she didn't like her, it was clear that she knew Eleanor was someone to be reckoned with.

The Blamer

All emotionally abusive people tend to be blamers. But some people are so good at blaming that they deserve a special classification all their own.

Blamers are never wrong. Whenever there is a problem, it is always someone else's fault. If they ever do admit to having done something wrong, they will always justify it or rationalize it by trying to convince you that their abusive behavior is an understandable reaction to some terrible deficiency or provocation on your part. By shifting the blame to you, they protect themselves in two important ways: they absolve themselves of any role of wrongdoing, and they convince you that your character deficiencies are the real reason for the problems in the relationship. Any criticism or questioning of this is immediately turned back on you as further proof of your inadequacies. By always blaming others, blamers can avoid having to consider the possibility that they have any serious shortcomings.

ALAN: GASLIGHTING, EMOTIONAL BLACKMAIL   Alan was an alcoholic. He had been living with Starr for three years and had managed during that entire time to convince her that she was the reason why he drank. He told her he drank because she nagged at him too much, he drank because she never gave him any freedom, because she was so domineering. If he came home drunk late at night he said it was because he knew she'd be angry at him anyway for stopping at the bar, so he figured he might as well make an evening of it. He'd often start a fight with her just so he would have the excuse to stay out late drinking.

Starr felt guilty for nagging at Alan and being angry at him all the time so she believed him when he said he drank because of her. She became so afraid that he was going to get drunk and stay out late that she stopped saying anything to him that he might perceive as criticism. This didn't stop Alan from staying out late and getting drunk of course; he just found other excuses and other ways to blame Starr for his problems.

The Destroyer

These people are out to destroy their victims. Some do it consciously while others are totally unaware of their desire to destroy others. They may be misogynists, they may be jealous or envious, or they may be acting out the anger and hurt they suffered as children. Or, they may be projecting the self-hatred and self-loathing they feel for themselves onto those closest to them.

Some men deliberately set out to destroy every woman they get involved with. They may do this by learning her weaknesses and then exploiting them, by financially destroying her, or by making her doubt her desirability.

The following letter appeared in a recent Ann Landers column. It was written by a woman responding to an earlier letter from a young woman who had complained about her emotionally abusive fiancé:

This is what her life will be like if she marries him. Everything she does will make him angry. He will draw her into arguments so he can "win." She will say anything to avoid antagonizing him because he becomes so punitive. She will end up saying, "I don't know" or "I don't care" to every question. Her life will be hell.

She will stop seeing her friends and family because he will pick fights with everyone and ruin every evening. If she shows any joy or pleasure, he will find a way to punish her, so she will learn to be passive and neutral. If she expresses any negative feelings, he will tell her she is "crazy," "paranoid," and "neurotic."

The man this woman was describing is a destroyer. The destroyer deliberately tries to rob you of any avenue of pleasure, self-expression, or self-esteem. He wants to do more than control you—he wants to annihilate you.

BOBBY: GASLIGHTING   A destroyer who uses gaslighting techniques manipulates things to make you feel as if you are crazy, stupid, losing your memory, lazy, and so on. Such techniques can be used so cleverly that you may have a particularly difficult time realizing that you are being emotionally abused.

In the two years Sheila had known him, Bobby had systematically worked on destroying her. A compulsive liar, he fabricated tales about what she supposedly had said and done. He was so clever at making her doubt herself that she didn't know what was happening to her.

It had first started when Sheila and Bobby drank or smoked marijuana together. The next day, Bobby would tell Sheila that she had insulted one of their friends, or flirted with a man at the party, or had made a fool of herself. Sheila couldn't remember doing any of these things, but she had no reason to believe that Bobby would lie, so she assumed that she had probably been too drunk or too stoned to remember what she had done. She would apologize to Bobby and vow to not drink or smoke so much the next time. But even though she cut down on these things, Bobby convinced her that her behavior had not changed. He always seemed to have a hard time "forgiving" her, and he constantly threw things up at her that he claimed she had done to hurt him.

As time went by, Bobby started telling Sheila that she had said certain things she didn't remember saying, or had gone places with him that she didn't remember going to. He teased her so much about her having a bad memory that she finally believed that she did.

Sheila became more and more convinced that she must be crazy. How else could she explain her uncharacteristic behavior and her seeming lack of awareness of herself? As is the case with many women who are being emotionally abused, Sheila started therapy because she was afraid she was going crazy. In therapy, Sheila slowly began recounting all the things that Bobby had accused her of, sorting out reality from the lies.

But it would have taken her a lot longer to begin to believe in herself again and to see the truth about Bobby if it hadn't been for a phone call she received from one of Bobby's ex-girlfriends. This woman, Caroline, warned Sheila of Bobby's pattern of emotionally abusing the women he was involved with. Caroline told Sheila that Bobby had come into her life while she was recovering from a head injury following a car accident. As is typical of trauma victims, Caroline couldn't remember the car accident or a great deal of what had occurred just before it. In addition, because of her head injury, she was often disoriented and confused.

At first, Bobby had been wonderful to her, taking her to the doctor, cooking and cleaning for her and reassuring her that she would be okay. Then he gradually began to deliberately confuse her. When she would return home from seeing a friend, Bobby would ask, "Where are the groceries?" Then, when Caroline would ask, "What groceries?" he would look at her intently and say very slowly, "Caroline, don't you remember that you told me you were going to the grocery store?" Caroline would become very upset and insist that she had told him she was going to see a friend. Bobby would just look at her as though she were crazy and shake his head back and forth, saying, "Okay, Caroline, whatever you say."

Caroline also told Sheila that Bobby had used her lack of memory against her, insinuating that the reason she had "forgotten" what had happened just before the accident was that she had probably done something horrible she didn't want to remember.

Caroline's parents saw that she was declining rapidly, and they became concerned that Bobby was doing her some harm. They tried to get her to come stay with them for a while, but she didn't want to leave Bobby. Finally, they had a private investigator check out Bobby's past to see whether their fears were warranted. It turned out that Bobby did, indeed, have a sordid past, full of scandal and deception. There was a long string of women who had been emotionally and sometimes financially destroyed by him. Fortunately, Sheila believed Caroline and was able to leave Bobby before he completely destroyed her.

Dr. Jekyll and Mr. Hyde

At times this type of emotional abuser is gentle, loving, caring, and generous, and at other times he is snarling, brutish, and mean. He can be the nicest guy in the world or the meanest SOB you ever met. These people can experience extreme mood swings, going from elation to depression in a very short time. Sometimes their mood swings are caused by alcohol or drugs. When clean and sober they may be brilliant, caring, and responsible, but when drinking or using drugs they become irrational, cruel, and irresponsible. Other times their mood swings are a symptom of an emotional disturbance.

SHARON: UNPREDICTABLE BEHAVIOR, VERBAL ABUSE   Sharon and Billie are lesbian lovers who have been together for two years. While Billie wants desperately to be with Sharon, she is getting to the point where she feels that she may be forced to leave her. Billie explained to me what it is like living with Sharon:

> Sharon can be the most loving and generous person you'd ever want to meet. She has been there for me when I've really needed her and I'll always be grateful to her for that. But she can also be a raving maniac who becomes so angry and so abusive that sometimes I think she's going to drive me crazy. For no apparent reason she gets into a mood where she starts picking at me about everything I do. Once she starts in on me she doesn't stop for days. She yells at me for hours on end, and follows me around the house berating me for something she

imagines I have done. She keeps bringing up things that happened months or years ago that I thought we had already resolved.

Then, when I think I am just about to go crazy she stops as suddenly as she starts. She apologizes for misjudging me and cries and tells me how wonderful I am to put up with her. I know I should probably leave her. She refuses to get any help and I think she needs it. On the other hand, I don't know who needs help more—her or me. Why do I keep staying with someone who is so erratic? I must have a screw loose myself, don't you think?

I assured Billie that she was not crazy but I did tell her that I was concerned about her emotional well-being. I explained to her that she was being emotionally abused and that whether Sharon could help her erratic mood swings or not, she was damaging Billie with her behavior. Billie and I worked together for several months before she was finally able to end this potentially dangerous relationship.

SOME UNHEALTHY MATCHES

Emotionally abused women are drawn to emotional abusers like moths to the flame. While an emotionally abused woman can be attracted to any number of abusive types, some particular attractions seem to occur time and time again. Following are some examples of these matches made in hell.

The Selfless Woman and the Narcissist

It makes sense that the selfless woman be attracted to a narcissist, who appears to have the qualities she lacks—self-confidence and a willingness to take risks. Having a tendency to fantasize a great deal herself, the selfless woman easily gets caught up in the narcissist's illusionary world of fantasies and dreams and buys into his grandiose self-image. Because she has few interests of her own, she is easily caught up in the life of the narcissist, who demands her total attention and adoration. She gets lost in him, and he loves it. He is strongly opinionated, and she goes along with all of his opinions and ideas. Because the selfless woman has a fear of being smothered, she feels comfortable with the narcissist, who is also incapable of true intimacy. Unfortunately, many selfless women interpret the Narcissist's lack of interest in them and tendency to devalue them as evidence that they are uninteresting and unimportant. Even though her self-esteem is being greatly damaged, because she is so afraid of being alone the selfless woman will probably not leave the narcissist unless he rejects her so completely that her pride forces her to finally let go.

As time goes on, however, the selfless woman may begin to see the narcissist for who he really is. If she stands up to him, he will feel insulted and become enraged, accusing her of no longer believing in him and of not supporting him. He will become even more defensive and bent on making her doubt her perceptions.

She will either buckle under again or she will begin to see through his defenses. She in turn will then begin to devalue him—since he is not all good he is therefore all bad. She will feel trapped and critical, feeling as if she is with an imposter and that the entire relationship was a hoax. She will feel like she is with a stranger—as if she really never knew him at all and will chastise herself for being such a fool.

In addition, even though she does not value herself, she may eventually resent the fact that he obviously does not value her. She will get tired of the fact that his needs, his ideas, and his feelings are all important and that he seldom, if ever, has time to listen to her or take an interest in what she is doing.

The Pleaser and the Controller

Because a pleaser is so agreeable, so complacent, and so eager to please, she is very attractive to a controller. He will think he has died and gone to heaven when he realizes just how willing she is to do his bidding. And since the pleaser is often attracted to men like her own controlling father, this combination occurs often.

In some ways these two people would seem to be fairly compatible, but since the controller can never be pleased, the pleaser will become more and more frustrated. And since she already suffers from low self-esteem and depends on the approval of others to make her feel worthwhile, her self-esteem will suffer even further from being around a controller. Although she wants to please and will seldom stand up for herself, the pleaser doesn't really want to be controlled and will eventually begin to feel abused.

The more a controller is allowed to control others, the more domineering he becomes. He will want to control her every move and she, in her attempts to please him, will allow him to control her so much that she will lose all sense of independence, self-respect, and sense of self.

The Sinner and the Blamer

The sinner believes she needs to make up for her past wrongdoings by being good now. The blamer believes that he is perfect and everyone else is wrong. Together, these two keep each other's neuroses going: the more he blames her, the worse she feels about herself, and the more she tries to make it up to him. The more she tries to please him, the more he blames her for his problems and inadequacies. He has a readily available target for all his rage and anger; she has constant proof that she is bad.

This is obviously a very destructive coupling, especially for the sinner. Many sinners become chronically ill after living with a blamer for awhile. Others, already plagued with self-doubt, guilt, and shame, may grow to feel so bad about themselves that they become suicide risks. And since the blamer has someone so readily available to hold responsible for all his problems, he is never required to look at his own problems. In the meantime, whether his problems include alcoholism, gambling, overeating, procrastinating, or an inability to get along with others, they will worsen with time, creating for some blamers a life-threatening situation.

The Victim and the Destroyer

Looking for someone to rescue her, the victim is fooled by the destroyer, who can easily pass himself off as a rescuer. Once he has won her over, this "knight in shining armor" will turn out to be far more dangerous to his victim than whatever catastrophe he has "saved" her from.

The destroyer will discover and exploit the victim's weaknesses, systematically tearing down any self-confidence she has. She will become more and more dependent upon him and will stay to suffer more abuse because she feels powerless to walk away.

A good example of a victim/destroyer combination is Hedda Nussbaum and Joel Steinberg. Throughout the years Joel systematically destroyed Hedda by dominating and controlling her, by using gaslighting techniques to make her believe she was crazy, with his cruelty and finally his physical violence.

The Codependent and the Antisocial Personality

The codependent woman will often be attracted to an antisocial male because she wants to reform or "fix" him. As noted earlier, antisocial people are often in trouble with the law; many are alcoholics, drug addicts, or compulsive gamblers or else display other compulsive behaviors. The antisocial person's problems and weaknesses are actually attractive to a codependent and are, in fact, what keep the relationship going.

As long as she can focus on trying to reform him, the codependent does not have to face her own problems. His behavior is so obviously unacceptable that any inappropriate behavior on her part seems minimal by comparison.

The codependent finds something so compelling about a person who needs "fixing" that she will be sucked back into the relationship time after time, no matter how destructive the relationship ends up being. The antisocial personality only need promise her he will "try harder" or "be better," and the codependent woman falls for it every time. She doesn't want to see that he has no intention of stopping his addictive, compulsive, or abusive behavior.

The Drama Junkie and Dr. Jekyll/Mr. Hyde

The drama junkie will be very attracted to the unpredictable and moody Dr. Jekyll and Mr. Hyde personality. Often addicted to drugs or alcohol, this type of emotional abuser creates the constant chaos, drama, and excitement that the drama junkie craves.

Sexuality undoubtedly plays an important role in this relationship. Because the Dr. Jekyll and Mr. Hyde often alternates between being affectionate and close, and being cold and distant, the drama junkie never knows where she stands. He may alternate between being totally disinterested in sex and being insatiable. While many people would find this situation unbearable, the drama junkie is turned on to her partner's changeableness—she can't take him for granted and she never knows which mood he'll be in. In fact, his emotional distance may hold the highest appeal. Constantly looking for a challenge, trying to interest her mate in sex when he is in one of his nonsexual moods may be the ultimate in excitement for the drama junkie.

While most other types of emotionally abused women may finally be able to break away from a Dr. Jekyll and Mr. Hyde, the drama junkie will become so addicted to his mood changes that she will not be able to get away. After all, he is an ever-present provider of the drama fixes she so desperately needs.

In this chapter you've met possessors, Napoleons, bulldozers, controllers, sex addicts, antisocial personalities, narcissists, misogynists, blamers, destroyers, and Dr. Jekyll/Mr. Hydes. You may have also seen yourself in reading other women's stories. It is extremely painful to realize that you have been victimized by an emotional abuser, and it can feel very humiliating. But remember: *you are not alone*. There are thousands of other women who have been, or still are, in your shoes. Remember, too, that you have to crawl before you can walk. Admitting that you are a victim of emotional abuse is the first step toward recovery, a recovery that you most certainly deserve and can accomplish. You cannot change the emotional abuser, but you *can* change yourself.

UNDERSTANDING YOURSELF: THE KEY TO CHANGE

CHAPTER 4

Why Are You Attracted to Emotional Abusers?

Even though I'm thirty-three, I still feel like a child. My life is a disaster. I keep going through the same thing all the time. I make a friend, and she ends up being overly critical of me or hurting me in some way. I get a new job, and I end up getting a boss who is too demanding. Sometimes I feel as though I never left home—like my domineering, controlling father is following me all through my life.

What's wrong with me? I can't believe I've done it again. I thought that this time I had gotten involved with a good guy, someone who really loved me. But he's just like all the rest of the jerks I've known. Why do I keep doing this to myself? When am I ever going to learn? I fall in love and have high hopes that this person will be the one, but he never is. I always find out that he's just using me, like all the rest.

This kind of verbal self-flagellation is common among emotionally abused women. We just can't believe that we keep doing the same things over and over, that we keeping getting into emotionally abusive relationships that leave us feeling hurt, angry, ashamed, fearful, confused, and—most of all—stupid.

Instead of putting yourself down and mentally beating yourself up for making yet another mistake in your choices of people, it will be far more productive for you to begin looking at *why* you choose abusive people in the first place.

Because the chances are extremely high that you were emotionally, physically, and/or sexually abused as a child, you have been programmed to seek out abusive types of people. In this section we will explore exactly how your past has set you up for further abuse.

The emotional abuse you sustained as a child continues to affect you in many ways. One of the most obvious effects is seen in your attraction to emotionally abusive people. Once such a person has become part of your life, you find it extremely difficult to get away from him. Those of us who were emotionally abused as children are far more likely to stay in abusive situations than those who were not. Even if you *are* able to escape, you soon find yourself in yet another abusive relationship.

Why Do You Choose Abusers?

There are several reasons why you may seem to repeatedly find yourself in abusive situations, and why you stay in them too long. The most notable reasons are these:

- ☐ You are used to being treated poorly.
- ☐ You had poor modeling by your mother and other female caretakers.
- ☐ You have low self-esteem.
- ☐ You are reenacting earlier abuse.

Let's consider each of these reasons in detail.

"I'm Used to It"

Women who have been raised in healthy families expect to be treated with consideration, respect, and kindness, and they reject people who treat them otherwise. As a victim of childhood abuse, however, you are accustomed to being treated with indifference, disrespect, or cruelty, and you may even have come to believe that such treatment is natural.

If you grew up in an atmosphere of continual upheaval and emotional outbursts, constant bickering, inconsistent responses, or alcohol or drug abuse, you are accustomed to chaos and drama. You may even be addicted to it, actually feeling uncomfortable when things are peaceful. In addition, you may even be attracted to physical violence, possessiveness, and cruelty in others, getting a strong emotional charge from being possessed, dominated, and even physically abused.

"What *Role Models?*"

Not only do we often become attracted to people who are like our abusive parent was, but because of the role-modeling our parents provided we often repeat the pattern of their marriage, acting out their "scripts." My client Robin explained her situation:

> My father was clearly the one in charge. My mother seemed to be defined by him. Her whole life was centered around what he wanted from her, and she waited on him hand and foot. If she pleased him she was rewarded by his affection, but if she angered him he would withdraw and not speak to her.
>
> It is amazing to me to see that I have done the same thing, giving my husband all the power in our relationship. My self-worth has been determined by whether or not I please him. And I'll be damned if I didn't marry a man who punishes me just like my father punished my mother. He stops talking to me and becomes very withholding.

Your mother may have taken on the role of peacemaker or placater to your verbally abusive or violent father. Acting as a kind of half-person, she tried to smooth his ruffled feathers. She didn't make waves, didn't ask questions, didn't want to know what was really going on. You, in turn, may have taken on the same role when you grew up, becoming passive, helpless, and dependent.

Allison told her support group how she came to realize that she had modeled herself after her mother:

> I know this is hard to believe, but I actually made excuses for the fact that my husband was a womanizer who had numerous affairs. I told myself that I probably wasn't a good lover, that I wasn't pretty or

desirable enough, and that because he was a good husband in most other respects I should just ignore it.

　　But in therapy it became clear just why I was putting up with this unacceptable behavior. When I was a child I watched my mother put up with all kinds of abusive behavior from my father. She always made excuses for him and usually blamed herself in some way. She taught me by her example that no matter how unacceptable or how abusive your husband is, you have to put up with it because a woman really can't make it on her own.

By watching your mother, you also learned what educational and job possibilities were open to you. You may have learned from her that women have very limited options. If your mother was a housewife, you were probably taught that your security lay in getting a man to support you. If your parents could afford to send you to college, you may have been encouraged to become a teacher, a nurse, or a social worker, perhaps like your mother. You probably learned that you should also defer to men at work, and that no matter how oppressive a boss was, you should keep your mouth shut and be happy you had a job at all.

"I Can't Get Anything Better, Anyway"

Because their self-esteem was so damaged by childhood abuse, many women don't feel they deserve to be treated well. Instead of rejecting those who treat them poorly, they accept the behavior without question. Some women are so filled with shame and self-loathing that they don't believe they deserve any better than the treatment they are getting, no matter how abusive it is. Even if they recognize the abuser's behavior as inappropriate, they feel they have to settle for what they can get because they don't believe they can get anything better.

　　Many women were so severely rejected or criticized as children that they assume that there is something wrong with them and that they are not ever going to be accepted and loved for who they are. This is what happened to Val:

　　Val had been very sexually promiscuous ever since she began dating. In high school she had wanted a boyfriend very badly, because she thought it was the way to be accepted. She thought that the only way a boy would want to date her was if she had sex with him.

As she grew older, her already low self-esteem became even shakier, since most of the men she dated just used her sexually and then never called again. Val became more and more needy for affection and would subject herself to all kinds of abuse and degradation in order to be held and touched for just a few minutes.

> I thought that if I pleased them, they would love me. But no matter what I did for them sexually, I was never going to get their approval and love. I know that now, but at the time I didn't understand, because I had been raised in a home where everything was done for the males in the family. My mother, my sister, and I would wear ourselves out catering to my father and brothers. I know now that by having sex with all those men I was still trying desperately to get my father's approval in the only way I knew how, by making myself a slave. But just like my father and brothers, these men never really appreciated what I gave to them.

Many women with low self-esteem are attracted to men who seem strong and self-assured. But because these women lack self-confidence themselves, they are ill-equipped to recognize true self-assuredness and are thus easy prey for the charlatan, the phony who puts up a facade of self-confidence and strength. Too often, these women mistake machismo, dominance, and a need to control for self-assuredness, strength, and assertiveness.

"This Time I'll Get it Right!"

Women who continually get involved with abusive people may be unconsciously, or perhaps even consciously, attempting to rewrite the past. For example, if we couldn't get our parents to love us, we become involved with people very much like our parents and try to make *them* love us. We develop patterns of relating to people based on our futile attempts to master and change what has already happened.

My own pattern was to continually get involved with female friends who were critical, demanding, unreasonable, and selfish. While I did have some friends who treated me with kindness and generosity, I always seemed to be particularly attracted to the other type. I put far more effort into friendships with people who treated me poorly, trying in vain to make them more appreciative of me, than I did into the friendships with people who were already accepting and generous.

I was shocked when I finally discovered, years later, that I was choosing friends who treated me like my mother had. I had been determined to change them, to make them give me what my mother had never given me. Although I had long since given up trying to change my mother, I had simply transferred this struggle into my friendships.

Freud called this tendency to reenact our past the "repetition compulsion." Author Judith Viorst writes about this compulsion in her classic book *Necessary Losses:* "Thus, whom we love and how we love are revivals—unconscious revivals—of early experience, even when revival brings us pain. . . . We will act out the same old tragedies unless awareness and insight intervene."

DISCOVERING YOUR ORIGINAL ABUSERS

Because most emotionally abused women are indeed propelled into abusive relationships because of the repetition compulsion, trying desperately to get what they didn't get as children, reenacting their past abuse in a futile attempt to change the past, it is important to discover who your original abuser is. While several different people may have emotionally abused you as a child, there is more than likely one or two of these abusers who stand out in your mind. These are the people who have damaged you the most, who most influenced who you are today. These are your original abusers.

Original abusers are not always the first person to have abused you but they are the first person to have caused significant, lasting damage to you by their abuse. More than likely your original abuser was one or both of your parents since parents have a more profound effect on our lives than anyone else.

Just as you were not necessarily aware that you were being emotionally abused as an adult, you are probably not cognizant of the fact that you were emotionally abused as a child. Often we grow up thinking that the way we were treated was normal and to be expected when in fact it was abusive. Emotional abuse of children includes physical neglect, emotional neglect or deprivation, abandonment, verbal abuse, emotional sexual abuse, boundary violation, role reversal, chaotic abuse (being raised in an environment where there is constant upheaval and discord and very little stability), social abuse (when parents directly or indirectly interfere with their child's access to her peers or fail to teach their child essential social skills), and intellectual abuse (when a child's thinking is ridiculed or attacked and she is not allowed to differ from her parent's point of view).

While there isn't room in this book for an in-depth exploration of the different types of emotionally abusive parents, the following brief descriptions will help you to discover whether one or both of your parents were your original abuser(s).

The Possessive Parent

The possessive parent wants to control, own, and consume her child. She begins when her child is an infant, overprotecting her, holding her so close that her child may feel suffocated. When her child reaches the age where she wants to begin exploring the world separate from her parent, the possessive parent feels threatened and clings to her child even tighter. This behavior continues throughout childhood, with the parent feeling jealous of anything and anyone that threatens to take away her child. For example, the parent may discourage her child from making friends by always finding fault with each of her child's playmates. Instead of beginning to loosen the reins a little bit as her child becomes older and more mature, she may become even more strict, insisting on knowing at all times where her child is going and with whom. When her child begins to take an interest in dating, the parent may become especially threatened and may either forbid her child to date or make her feel that no one is good enough for her.

Many fathers find having a daughter a very satisfying and rewarding experience until she reaches adolescence. Then he must deal with his daughter's sexuality and curb any incestuous thoughts he may have. Oftentimes a father is possessive of his daughter because he is sexually aroused by her and wants no other man to have her. He will forbid his daughter to date or will be horrified when she wears anything that is the slightest bit revealing.

Some parent's possessiveness comes from a need to protect their daughter from harm. For example, if they themselves were sexually abused as a child, they may assume that all men are capable of sexually molesting their daughter. Some men who have these impulses themselves or who have been promiscuous or used women sexually assume that every boy who dates their daughter is going to use her sexually.

Other parents do not want their daughter to grow up because they want her to be available to take care of their needs. These parents may not have gotten their needs met by their mothers or spouses and may in turn expect their daughter to meet those unmet needs. Still others become too attached to their daughter because they are widowed, divorced, or having difficulties with their spouse. If a parent treats his or her daughter like a confidante or a friend, he or she is being abusive. It is not a daughter's role to make her parents feel good or listen to their problems (sexual and otherwise).

The Overcontrolling Parent

Overcontrolling parents will attempt to control not only their children but their spouse as well. They behave in inflexible, even cruel ways, expecting everyone in the family to bow down to them and do as they say. This type of parent believes strongly in rules and obedience and that parents' authority should never be questioned—no matter what. They attempt to dominate their children completely, needing to feel in control over others in order to feel powerful and important. Often raised by overcontrolling parents themselves, they are often ventilating the anger they could not express to their own parents onto their children.

A girl growing up with an overcontrolling parent hears a barrage of commands, orders, and suggestions about anything and everything—what foods to eat, how to eat them, what clothes to wear, what classes to take in school, what boys to date. She will not be allowed to make her own decisions and any that she does manage to make will always be considered wrong.

Kim's father had to be in control of everything that went on in the household: "My mother and I couldn't do anything without checking with Dad first. We had to ask permission to buy clothes and then when we returned from a shopping trip he had to see all the receipts. He always had to meet all my friends and when I got older he would interrogate my boyfriends before he'd let me go out with them. He was the one who decided what college I went to and even what I majored in."

The Abandoning, Rejecting Parent

Parents can abandon their children *physically* (leaving them solely in the care of babysitters, leaving them home alone, having them wait in the car for hours at a time, forgetting to pick them up at the movies, or because of a divorce, leaving the house and seldom seeing them again) or *emotionally* (being emotionally unavailable to their children, depriving their children of the necessary attention, affection, and encouragement they need).

Parents who escape into alcohol, drugs, sleep, television, or books also abandon their children because they are essentially not there for them emotionally. Elizabeth told me the painful story of how it felt to be raised by a mother who was detached from her. "My mother is just never present, if you know what I mean. You just can't connect with her. When I was a child it was extremely painful to be around her because I always felt so empty and alone even in her presence. She didn't take an interest in anything I did or listen to anything I ever said. She reminded me of a ghost sometimes, kind of floating around, never really touching ground. Most of the time she had her head stuck in a book, off in some fantasy world. In many ways I feel like I never had a mother. Instead I had this robot who would cook for us and clean the house and do the laundry but couldn't really talk to us or hold us."

Many fathers, while physically present in the home, are passive and not actively involved with their children. Laurel describes her relationship with her father as a "nonrelationship." "He was there, but he seldom talked to me except to say goodnight or to nod if my mother told him something about me. He just wasn't interested in me or what I was doing. I knew I wasn't important to him, that I was just a mouth to feed."

In addition to being unresponsive, some parents are also unaffectionate. Anita shared with me, "I can't remember my father hugging or kissing me. Even to this day he seems very uncomfortable with affection. I hugged him at my graduation from college and he stiffened up so much that I felt terribly rejected and embarrassed.

"I loved my father and couldn't understand why my love for him wasn't returned. I kept wondering what was wrong with me and I kept trying to be a better daughter so he'd love me." Not having her father's time, attention, or direction, Anita felt worthless and assumed that there was something wrong with her, otherwise her father would have wanted to be with her.

The Hypercritical Parent

Hypercritical parents focus a tremendous amount of negative attention on their child. They find fault with almost everything the child does and keep a "hypervigilant," critical eye on their child, assuming the child is going to do something wrong any moment. Instead of complimenting their daughter for what she was able to accomplish or for what she did right, an overly critical parent will be quick to point out what their child has left undone or what she did wrong. The hypercritical parent continually finds fault with their child's looks, the way she talks, the way she interacts with others, her schoolwork, her child's choice of friends. Their child can never be polite enough, thoughtful enough, smart enough, or pretty enough to please them.

This type of parent may be overly critical of all their children, may be a misogynist and therefore only critical of her female children, or may single out only one child to be critical of (because the child reminds her of herself, the child's father, or her own mother). Or, she or he just may be a critical person in general, seeing the world through harsh, judgmental eyes.

Priscilla shudders when she talks about what it was like growing up with her hypercritical father. "He was always finding something wrong with one of us girls. Dinner time was one of the worst times because we were all there at the table for my father to inspect, and he always found something that wasn't to his liking. My sister was eating too noisily, I wasn't holding my fork right, my other sister wasn't eating enough, I was eating too much. We just couldn't do anything right. Before we had a chance to finish our meal my dad would slam his fist down hard on the table and order one of us to our room, yelling, 'Get out of my face!'"

Critical words to a child are as painful and as damaging as being physically hit. They are verbal slaps in the face, and usually accompanying the criticism are threats, name-calling, and yelling. This verbal abuse can be especially damaging. Insulting names echo in a child's mind over and over until she progresses to believing that she is indeed stupid, ugly, selfish, or lazy, and that in fact, that is *all* she is.

Any criticism from a parent carries with it the threat of losing the love of those on whom the child is totally dependent. A hypercritical parent continually threatens their child's sense of security and has a tremendous effect on their child's developing sense of self. Failing to balance their criticism with praise, they foster low self-esteem. This continual criticism can be so emotionally damaging to a child that it may take a lifetime to overcome. A child looks to her parents for approval, acceptance, and validation, so such approval is the most important thing she needs and strives for. A young child's entire life is centered around her parents and what they think of her. What her parents think of her will influence how she sees herself, how she assumes others see her, and how she sees other authority figures (as critical, threatening, or accepting).

When a girl's parents are hypercritical of her it causes her to be extremely sensitive to what others think of her, hypersensitive to even constructive criticism from others, critical of herself, and critical of others. Extreme criticism coming from a parent destroys the child's self-confidence, damages her self-esteem, thwarts her natural curiosity and sense of discovery of the world, and takes away her spontaneity.

The Alcoholic Parent

Alcoholism affects one out of every 10 Americans and there are an estimated 28 million children of alcoholics. Because of these numbers we know that a great deal of those who were emotionally abused as children were from alcoholic homes. Children of alcoholics are emotionally abused in a number of ways, most notably by being neglected physically and emotionally, abandoned, and verbally abused, by having to take on responsibilities before they are mature enough to do so, and by suffering unpredictability and a chaotic home environment.

The alcoholic parent is emotionally unavailable to his children most of the time, especially when he is drinking. Children of alcoholics are deprived of love and stability, for it is impossible for them to get their basic needs met by either the alcoholic parent or the codependent parent. Neither is able to give their child the love she needs. In addition, alcoholics are unpredictable, since they typically undergo an extreme behavior change when they begin to get drunk. Because of the chronic distress in an alcoholic family, children become hypervigilant, anxious, and chronically afraid.

Joyce experienced her mother's emotional unavailability, unpredictability, and verbal abuse when she was drunk:

> I looked forward to my mother coming home from work. I was a latch-key kid with no other siblings so I was really lonely. But from the time she got home she began to drink, and she continued to drink all night long until she finally staggered to bed. Sometimes she was a happy drunk and we'd sit and watch TV, even getting up and dancing to some of the old musicals together. But other times she began to get extremely critical the more drunk she became. She would start to pick on me, complaining that I never did anything around the house, or I didn't respect her enough, or I was getting too big for my britches. It was hard to respect someone who was slurring their words, falling over, or knocking over lamps.

When I was in high school we would get into verbal and physical fights because I didn't respect her and wouldn't automatically do what she said when she was drunk. If it didn't make any sense to me I wouldn't do it. Often, when she would start one of her tirades I would go into my bedroom to get away from her but she wouldn't leave me alone. She'd keep coming in and yelling at me until I would finally break down in tears. Then she'd get all sentimental and try to be close to me, giving me slobbery kisses. In one evening she could go from being jovial, to critical, to abusive, to overly sentimental.

Alcoholic families foster every kind of abuse. Because alcohol lowers inhibitions, physical, sexual, and emotional abuse are commonplace in alcoholic families. Some estimates say that two-thirds of adult children of alcoholics are physically violated and that 50 percent of incest fathers are alcoholic. Children of alcoholics are dragged into bars, driven around by a drunk driver, left in cars all night outside bars, exposed to and sometimes left with strangers of questionable backgrounds and intentions, and given alcohol or drugs by their parents.

Children of alcoholics grow up watching one out-of-control person trying to control another. They get caught up in the needs of both parents and thus become codependents. Codependency is an unconscious addiction to another person's dysfunctional behavior or a tendency to put other people's needs before your own. Children of alcoholics are robbed of their childhood since often they are required to take care of their alcoholic parents as well as their siblings and the household. Many adult children of alcoholics are plagued by a sense of failure for not having been able to save their parents from alcohol and some blame themselves for their parents' drinking.

There is very little real discipline in an alcoholic family. Instead of disciplining a child for misbehaving or in order to help the child improve, parents discipline out of irritation and rage about their own life. Most of the time it has nothing to do with the child. Without proper discipline, children grow up with poor impulse control, insufficient boundaries, and little willpower. This sets the stage for them to suffer from alcoholism, drug abuse, compulsive overeating, compulsive gambling, and other compulsive and addictive behaviors.

As Claudia Black, a noted expert on adult children of alcoholics, stated in her book, *It Will Never Happen To Me!*, alcoholic parents teach their children three rules: "Don't talk, don't trust, and don't feel." Adult children of alcoholics grow up suffering from various forms of denial. They deny how bad their childhoods were, deny that they were abused, and deny that they are still in pain. Because of this denial, they tend to be attracted to others who, like themselves, tend to deny their feelings and reality. This attraction, in addition to their tendency to be codependents and caretakers, is why so many adult children of alcoholics marry alcoholics and others suffering from compulsive disorders.

Because of the constant disruption in an alcoholic family, adult children of alcoholics also tend to be drama junkies. Accustomed to frequent crises and emergencies, they find themselves depressed and anxious when life is stable and uneventful. For this reason, they stir things up whenever life is too calm or when relationships with others are good. They are also attracted to those who are addicted to excitement too, thus setting the stage for lives that are in constant upheaval.

The Silent Partner

A silent partner is a parent who stands by and does nothing while the other parent sexually, physically, or emotionally abuses their child. While the term was originally used to refer to a mother who remained passive while her husband sexually abused their child, the phrase can also apply to a parent of either sex who doesn't attempt to stop the abusive parent from continuing the abusive behavior, no matter what form it takes.

In a recent Ann Landers column, a woman wrote of how she had chosen to remain silent about the fact that her husband was sexually abusing their children rather than face the wrath of her husband and the humiliation of exposure. In her words, "I was too embarrassed to say anything and let everyone know what was going on in our family." Because of her silence, this woman was responsible for her children's being sexually brutalized during their entire childhood.

Another reader wrote in response to this woman's letter. Her letter read in part:

> That miserable excuse for a mother took what was the easy way out for her, forcing her innocent children to bear the burden of her cowardice, a burden from which they will never be entirely free.
>
> My father abused me sexually for years. My mother knew and did nothing.
>
> I am old now and have come a long way from the mute, terrified emotional cripple I once was. And I've come most of the way alone. Remnants of that legacy from my parents, however, are with me to this day. I have never been able to trust a man or have a genuinely friendly relationship with another woman, which is a terrible way to live.
>
> Signed,
>
> Permanently scarred

When a mother allows her husband to hurt her or her daughter, she is teaching her daughter to turn the other cheek and be submissive. In her passivity she thus deprives her daughter of adequate parenting every bit as much as her abusive husband. By doing nothing to protect herself or her daughter, she leaves her daughter no option but to incorporate her father's cruelty along with her pseudohumility as role models.

Whenever a parent refuses to respond to his or her child's pleas for help and rescue her from the tyranny or abuse of the other parent, that parent is a passive participant in the injury. Loretta, whose mother was an extremely abusive woman, got little support from her father. By failing to protect himself and his children from her outbursts and abuse, he became his wife's accomplice. Loretta grew up despising weak men and instead became attracted to those who were outspoken and seemingly strong. Unfortunately, they were also bullies who tried to control her.

The Misogynistic Parent

This parent looks down upon and devalues females. Probably raised by misogynistic parents, he or she strongly believes that females are inferior to males and that because of this males have the right to control females. The misogynistic parent may also have a tremendous amount of anger toward females, either because he or she was emotionally, physically, or sexually abused by them or because he or she lost respect for them because they allowed others to abuse him or her.

A misogynistic mother will often show preferential treatment to her male children and ignore her female children. Misogynistic mothers are often filled with self-loathing and transfer this negativity to any female children they may have. Misogynistic parents may discourage their daughter from exhibiting weakness or vulnerability in any way, seeing these things as only proving females' inferiority.

Misogynistic mothers favor their sons to the extreme of being neglectful and indifferent toward their daughters. Raised to believe that males are superior beings to be catered to by the females in the family, these mothers pass on this belief to their daughters. This was the way it was when Helen was growing up. Raised on an isolated farm in Minnesota, she was the only female child out of nine. Surrounded by males, she longed to feel a special kinship with her mother. But instead of her mother having a soft spot in her heart for Helen, she made it clear to Helen that she preferred the male children. Helen was expected to wait on not only her father but on all her brothers as well. If she complained about all the work, her mother would tell her to shut up. If she sought her mother's comfort or understanding about a problem or if she went to her mother for affection, she would be pushed away or shunned.

ABUSE BY OTHER CARETAKERS AND AUTHORITY FIGURES

While parents certainly have the most influence over a child, other major caretakers, such as foster parents, stepparents, teachers, coaches, babysitters, grandparents, aunts, uncles, and religious leaders, can also have a tremendous amount of influence on a child's life since they are in positions of power and authority over the child and she looks up to them and sees them as role models. It is extremely abusive for those in authority to misuse that authority by ridiculing, or singling out any particular child. For example, teachers and coaches have been known to ridicule children for things the child has no control over—such as how she is dressed, what she looks like, how she is built, her accent, or her family's class status.

Sometimes teachers single out a particular child because of a personal prejudice. Nancy was emotionally abused by her high-school gym teacher, Miss White. When Nancy first entered therapy she was suffering from bulimia. Although she was of normal weight, she maintained it by binging and purging— stuffing herself with food to the point of being in pain and then forcing herself to throw up. She had started forcing herself to vomit after an extremely painful year of being ridiculed by Miss White.

Nancy was overweight and Miss White made no secret of the fact that she detested overweight people. Instead of taking her aside and trying to help her with her weight, she made her the laughingstock of her gym class. Whenever the students had to run laps around the field, Nancy would naturally lag behind the others. Miss White would yell at Nancy, "Come on Smith, move that fat ass of yours." And when Nancy would come dragging in, huffing and puffing, Miss White would say in front of everyone, "You wouldn't be so out of breath if you didn't have all that extra lard to carry around."

Children can encounter cruelty from caretakers and authority figures in the least likely of places and from the least likely of sources. Colleen had stuttered severely since she was a small child but her parents had never sought help for her problem. Now on her own, with a good job as a computer analyst, she sought therapy. I suspected abusive childhood incidents as a cause for her stuttering, but Colleen insisted that no such abuse had occurred. Since it is common for adults who were abused as children to block it from their memory, I kept digging. The story that finally emerged was a shocking one. It turned out that Colleen had been severely emotionally abused by a nun at the Catholic school she had attended.

Most of the nuns were very strict but Sister Margarite was the worst. If we ever said something we shouldn't have said she would wash our mouths out with soap and make us stand in the corner for the rest of the day. She even locked children in the closet for disobeying her. Every day we had to stand up in front of her class and recite a prayer or a scripture that we were supposed to have memorized. With a ruler in her hand, she would stand close to whoever was reciting and if the student made a mistake Sister Margarite would whack the ruler loudly on a desk. She had been known to rap students' knuckles when they disobeyed, so everyone was terrified of her ruler and the sound it made.

As Colleen told her story she suddenly remembered when she had begun to stutter.

I was so terrified of making a mistake that I began to stammer and stutter. That would make her angry and she'd whack that ruler. This would make me even more nervous of course and I'd stutter even more. Then she'd yell at me, "What's the matter with you? You sound like an imbecile! Begin again!" I'd become so terrified I'd finally burst out crying. Finally she'd let me sit down but not without a lecture about how stupid and lazy I was.

Abuse by Peers and Siblings

Adults are not the only ones who emotionally abuse children. Few people realize just how destructive children can be to their peers, how lasting the emotional damage of name calling and teasing can be. Indeed, children can be extremely cruel to one another. They make fun of fat kids, skinny kids, kids who are too short or too tall, too poor or too smart—in effect, they tease anyone who has an unusual physical feature or stands out from the crowd. We tend to just excuse kids' cruelty by laughingly saying, "Kids sure say it like it is," but children who have been made targets by other children's cruelty carry emotional scars well into adulthood.

Childhood teasing and bullying is extremely damaging to an individual's self-esteem. Many adults are still traumatized by the bullies of their past, still expecting to be treated poorly by their peers. Many grow up unable to trust their peers and feeling socially inadequate.

Time after time I hear stories from clients about how traumatized they were by other children. Some people are so severely affected that they are uncomfortable or even frightened when in the presence of children. One client told me that she cannot pass by a group of children playing without fearing that they will turn on her and call her names. "Here I am, an adult, and I am still afraid of bullies."

Sibling Rivalry Versus Sibling Abuse

While a certain amount of bickering between siblings is normal and should be expected, some parents seem to turn a blind eye to the overt abuse of one sibling by another, not recognizing it as such and minimizing the damage such abuse can cause. Instead of protecting the child who is being abused, they advise their children to work out their problems between themselves, something their children are clearly not equipped to do. In actuality, sibling abuse is a symptom of family dysfunction. Parents often set the stage for sibling abuse by shirking their responsibilities and forcing an older sibling to babysit or take sole responsibility for a younger one, thereby causing the older sibling to resent and feel burdened by the younger one. Feeling powerless to stand up to the parents, older siblings may misuse their position of authority over the younger child.

Other parents set up an abusive situation between siblings because of their obvious preference for or dislike of a particular child over the others. The preferred child will be resented by her siblings, setting the stage for her to be shunned or mistreated by them. A child who is disfavored or disliked by one or both of her parents (because she was born out of wedlock, because she reminds a parent of themself or an ex-mate, because she isn't as attractive, pretty, or outgoing as the others) is often the child who is also picked on by her siblings.

Sometimes parents make one child in the family "all good" and another child "all bad." Millie, considered to be the "problem child" in the family, remembers hearing her mother often tell others that her sister was such a wonderful child but that she was trouble from the day she was born.

> She always tells people that I cried and fussed all the time while my sister was a perfect baby, that I always talked back while my sister

always minded, and that I had trouble in school while my sister was an angel and a straight A student.

I was like the "bad seed" to my mother and this gave my sister Florence permission to treat me badly. She felt so superior to me that she felt like she had the right to criticize me and boss me around. She constantly complained about me to my parents. I felt like I was living with a spy. She even blackmailed me into letting her use my things and then would return them to me broken or damaged. If I said anything to her she would just deny it and say that I was the sloppy one and had done the damage myself. I felt so discounted, so misunderstood, and so furious with my mother for setting up this situation. I felt like a stranger in my own household with no one to turn to for understanding or comfort.

I guess it was inevitable that I would carry these feelings into my adulthood. Now I always treat my friends and boyfriends as if they are my enemy instead of my ally. It always feels like there is a battle or a competition going on and I seem to always feel like the loser. I resent other people's successes and I compete ferociously, as if my life depended upon it.

As you can see, your original abuser can be a parent, another caretaker or authority figure, a childhood bully, or a sibling—in essence, virtually anyone who had much contact with you or influence on you. You can have more than one original abuser, as is the case when both parents are emotionally abusive, and this may account for the fact that you have a pattern of being abused in two or three ways and by two or three different types of abusers.

I had two original abusers: my mother, and a man who sexually abused me when I was nine years old. I reenacted the emotional abuse by my mother by getting involved with friends who were critical and selfish, and I reenacted the sexual abuse by getting involved with men who were sex addicts.

If you are having difficulty discovering who your original abuser was, the following exercise can help:

1. Pick out one or two of the abusers from your childhood and make a list of the characteristics of each. On one half of the page, list the person's positive characteristics; on the other half, list the negative ones.

Example
My father:

NEGATIVES
selfish

demanding

critical and judgmental

an alcoholic

domineering and controlling

thinks he is always right

POSITIVES
good sense of humor

not educated but intelligent

My mother:

NEGATIVES
passive

dependent on my father

fearful and confused

blames herself for whatever
goes wrong

POSITIVES
generous

kind

2. Now list all the characteristics of the person or persons currently abusing you.

Example
My boyfriend:

NEGATIVES
always right

controlling

demanding

always wants things
his own way

hard to please

POSITIVES
ambitious

funny

intelligent

3. Compare the lists for your childhood abusers with the lists for your current abusers. Are there any similarities between the lists? Is there one childhood abuser who has many of the same characteristics as your current abuser(s)? In the examples shown, it is easy to see the similarities between the woman's boyfriend and her father.

4. Because you may be suffering emotional abuse from people other than those listed but not know it, make a list of the characteristics of *all* your current significant relationships— your boyfriend, your boss and coworkers, your friends and family members. Now compare these lists to the lists you have already made for current abusers and for childhood abusers. Do any of the people on the new lists share many of the qualities of your known abusers?

WHEN THERE IS MORE THAN ONE ABUSER IN YOUR LIFE

As I mentioned earlier, many women are emotionally abused by more than one person. Yet the type of abuse, and even the circumstances, can be remarkably similar.

Deborah came to see me because she and her live-in boyfriend, David, were having problems. Deborah blamed herself, saying that the main problem with the relationship was that she didn't trust David enough. He had even threatened to leave her because she was too suspicious.

> I don't know why, but I keep thinking he is seeing someone else. I get these calls in the middle of the night, and then the person hangs up. David is getting home from work later and later; he says he is working late, and he probably is but I just don't believe him. I have to admit I have gotten carried away and have even driven by his office to make sure his truck is parked outside. I guess it's my problem, but I just can't seem to get over the feeling that he's being unfaithful to me.

I saw Deborah for several weeks, during which time we worked on her "problem" of being too suspicious. As time went on, it became more and more clear to me that she did, indeed, have good reason to suspect David's behavior. There seemed to be too many discrepancies between what he told her at different times. In addition, the midnight phone calls increased, and David was getting home from work later and later. One time he even came home with lipstick on his shirt. But Deborah always ended up believing his excuses and feeling guilty for having been so suspicious.

I explored with Deborah why she might be suspicious of David in the first place. As it turned out, David had lied to her previously several times. For example, when they first met David had told her he had a great job that paid well, but after they moved in together she discovered that he was, in fact, unemployed and could just barely help with the rent.

Deborah finally began to accept that she was not to blame for all the problems in the relationship and that she had good reason to be suspicious. She confronted David one more time. As usual, he denied having an affair and tried to make her feel guilty about even suspecting him. Then he went into a tirade, yelling that she was never satisfied. After all, he'd gone out and gotten a job to please her. Now that he was working so hard, even working overtime so he could buy her nice things, she was suspicious of him. He said he just couldn't win, that she was just a demanding bitch.

This confrontation set Deborah back a bit, and she began to believe once again that she *was* being unreasonable. But it wasn't long before she had grown to a point at which she could no longer be fooled into blaming herself. One night, she was having dinner at a restaurant with a friend when she saw David walk by with his arm around another woman. This was the last straw, and Deborah ended the relationship with David almost immediately.

But Deborah also had other problems to deal with. Shortly after her breakup with David, she came into one of her sessions very upset about a fight she had just had with her boss.

Her boss, Andy, had promised her the world when she had first started working for him. She was to be totally in charge of the office. Andy had told her that even though he couldn't pay her a lot to start with, as the business got off the ground he would give her substantial raises.

However, the work load turned out to be far heavier than Andy had indicated. In addition, Deborah was expected to carry a beeper and be on call at all times. When she complained that her work load was just too much for one person and asked Andy to hire someone to help her, he first questioned why she needed help. He finally promised that he would hire someone to help, but he never did. Further, the promised raises never materialized.

One afternoon, Deborah was so swamped at work that she had finally had it. She marched into Andy's office and demanded that he get some help for her. Andy yelled at her that she was being a demanding bitch, and he berated her for disrupting the office.

Once again, Deborah immediately doubted herself, feeling that even though her complaints were legitimate, she had had no right to confront Andy as she did. "I really was being bitchy, you know, and I had no right to yell at him like I did," she told me sheepishly. I reminded her that it sounded as though Andy had been the one doing the yelling, and that confronting someone with a legitimate complaint was not being "bitchy."

During this session, Deborah realized that it had made her feel better to verbalize her complaints, and that Andy had just been shifting the blame to avoid being accountable for not having kept his promises to her. She also realized that both she and Andy knew that she was getting stronger and wouldn't be putting up with his abuse much longer.

The next day, Deborah walked into her office and found a note on her desk from Andy, telling her that her services were no longer needed. He had, in fact, hired her replacement, who was already there at the office, waiting for Deborah to leave.

I was struck by the similarities between the ways Deborah's boyfriend and her boss had treated her. Both had: offered her a lot of talk but no action, lied to her, and tried to shift the blame for their problems to her, accusing her of being unreasonable and trying to make her feel guilty. David had an affair with another woman, and Andy had hired someone else behind Deborah's back.

Both David and Andy could be classified as antisocial personalities. And, you may have guessed, both were very much like Deborah's original abuser, her father. When Deborah was a child, her father would spin fantastic tales of things he had done in his younger years. As an adult, Deborah realized that he couldn't possibly have done most of them, but as a child she had naturally believed him.

Her father also used to tell Deborah and her siblings that if they did all their chores and were good all week, he would take them somewhere special on the weekend—to the beach, the country, or an amusement park, for example. Deborah remembered waking up full of anticipation on the day of the outing. As soon as the family had piled into the car, however, Deborah's father would suddenly announce that they weren't going because one of the children hadn't completed a chore to his satisfaction. If anyone complained, he would become irate and start yelling that all of the kids were ungrateful brats who didn't deserve a good father like they had. Then they would all be sent to their rooms. Deborah's mother never spoke up for the children but instead cowered in the background.

Further, Deborah also remembered once having seen her father drive by with a woman she didn't know. Much later, she learned that her father had had numerous affairs.

Like David and Andy, Deborah's father had lied, made false promises and shifted the blame when he broke them, and had secret involvements with other people. Deborah was stunned when she was finally able to see the connections between the way her father had treated her and the way she was being abused in her adult life.

You can make connections between your past and your present, too.

Starting with your current life and tracing back as far as you can remember, list all the different people who have abused you. Next to each name, list the types of abuse that person inflicted upon you. (The listing of different types of emotional abuse in chapter 1 can help you.)

See if you can find some similarities, the way Deborah was finally able to do. If you discover that you have had a tendency to be abused in similar ways, this indicates that you are reenacting the relationship you had with an original abuser or abusers.

PATTERNS OF ABUSE

For the reasons discussed above, an emotionally abused woman often has a series of involvements with abusive people who are remarkably similar both to one another and to the original abuser(s). I will illustrate this point with a few case histories.

Client: Pam
Pattern:
Marrying someone like her mother

Type of abuse:
Unpredictable responses, constant chaos

Pam's husband, Duane, was very loving. He helped with the housework, and at least once a week he had dinner ready when Pam got home from work. He gave her frequent massages for her sore back. He often told her how beautiful she was, and he went out of his way to let her know he loved her, bringing her flowers and even serving her breakfast in bed every Sunday morning.

But every so often, Duane would change radically and blow up, telling Pam that he hated her and her family, that she was ugly and stupid, and that he wished he'd never married her. Once he told her that he had married her for her money, and another time he said he had married her because the woman he *really* loved had rejected him. The day after one of these blowups, Duane would be back to being his loving self. He would apologize, telling Pam that he hadn't meant any of what he had said and that he loved her very much. Pam told me, "It was like there were two Duanes—the loving, generous husband, and the raging monster."

As she was to discover in therapy, Pam had married a man who was very much like her mother. Pam's mother had gone out of her way to make sure her children had everything they needed and wanted. She was also very affectionate and loving, and she always took a real interest in her children's daily lives, listening attentively as they told her of their activities. But she also had another side to her, an angry, resentful side that would cause her to burst into uncontrollable rages. Without notice, she would blow up and tell her children that she wished she had never had them.

Client: Yvette
Pattern:
Marrying a man like her father and repeating her mother's behavior

Type of abuse:
Sexual harassment, gaslighting, emotional blackmail

Yvette's husband, Roger, was very sexually demanding. He wanted sex at least once, if not two or three times, each day. Yvette would have preferred to have sex two or three times a week. Roger insisted that Yvette didn't really love him—otherwise, he said, she would want to have sex as often as he did. This daily pressure was very difficult for Yvette.

> I began to feel edgy and nervous just anticipating his next approach. I could be doing anything, and he would come up to me and grab me. Then I'd push him away, and the accusations would begin: "You don't love me. . . . You're frigid. . . . Why can't you just do it for me?" It got so that I didn't want to go to bed at night for fear that he would try to get on top of me. The same was true of waking up in the morning.

Roger tried to make Yvette believe that there was something wrong with her because she didn't want to have sex every day, and because she didn't want to participate in certain sexual acts. She told me,

> I began to think there was something wrong with me, that maybe I was undersexed or something. Roger told me other wives enjoyed performing these acts with their husbands, and that I should, too. But as hard as I tried, I just couldn't bring myself to do some of these things. It made me physically sick just to think about them.

Finally, Roger began to threaten to go get sex from someone else.

> At first this scared me. I was afraid of losing him. I tried harder for several weeks to have sex with him as often as he wanted it, but he still wasn't satisfied. In fact, it seemed that the more I had sex with

him, the more he wanted it. I just couldn't keep up. After a while, whenever he threatened to go have sex with someone else, I started telling him to go ahead. It began to feel like a relief to me that he could get some of his needs met elsewhere.

Roger was a sex addict. He was addicted to sex in much the same way a person can be addicted to drugs, alcohol, gambling, or spending. His urge to have sex so often was based on a need for approval and a validation of his power and masculinity, not on a need for intimacy or on an unusually high sex drive. Like so many other sex addicts, Roger depended on sex to feel good about himself. In his mind, the only way Yvette could prove that she loved him was to be sexual with him.

Yvette's father had also been a sex addict. He had constantly pressured Yvette's mother about sex and had complained that she was "sexless" and didn't love him enough to take care of his needs. Unlike Roger, he hadn't just threatened to go out with other women; he had actually done it.

Now I understand my mother more. Everyone knew Daddy was going out with other women, and I couldn't understand why Momma put up with it. Now I think she was probably relieved, like I would be, not to be pressured into having sex all the time. I remember Daddy always telling me, "Don't end up like your mother. Make sure you please your husband—make sure you let him know how much you love him. That's the only way to keep a man. Believe me, if you don't make him happy at home, he'll go somewhere else."

Client: Amelia
Pattern:
A pleaser who tends to get involved with hypercritical people like her mother

Type of abuse:
Constant criticism, domination

Amelia's best friend, Lonnie, was always very critical of her. She criticized the way Amelia dressed, the way she wore her hair, the way she talked, and the men she dated. Since Amelia valued her friend's opinion, she usually took her suggestions to heart and tried to change herself accordingly.

> When I first met Lonnie, I didn't know how to dress. She took me under her wing and taught me what looked good on me. I also had horrible taste in men. You should have seen some of the losers I went out with! But now they all have to pass inspection with Lonnie before I'll go out with them twice.

It doesn't sound as though Amelia feels she is being emotionally abused, does it? After all, she welcomes her friend's input. But the problem is that Amelia is giving far too much power to Lonnie. Whenever we allow someone else to dictate how we should run our lives, we are giving our power away. Another problem is that Lonnie is never satisfied: even though Amelia does nearly everything she suggests, Lonnie continues to find fault. Although Amelia is not aware of it, her self-confidence is slowly being eroded, and she is gradually losing faith in her own perceptions and abilities. She has become dependent on Lonnie for advice, for decision making, and for approval. She is losing her self.

Not surprisingly, all during Amelia's childhood her mother had been extremely critical of her. No matter how hard Amelia tried, she just couldn't please her mother. Her mother was also extremely dominating, insisting on choosing all of Amelia's clothes and telling her what friends she could play with. Because she believed her mother knew best, and because she wanted so desperately to please her, Amelia followed all of her mother's advice explicitly.

Amelia didn't consider Lonnie's treatment of her to be abusive, because she was used to it from her mother. She was also blind to the fact that she was trying to get from Lonnie the approval she had never gotten from her mother. In other words, she was trying to redo the past.

The women you have met in this chapter were all unconsciously reenacting their relationships with their original abusers. Although like everyone else they only wanted to be loved, they were compelled to repeat the past in a desperate effort to master and change it, hoping each time they tried that somehow *this* time would be different.

Recognizing that you are repeating a pattern and are now with an abusive person much like your original abuser can be extremely liberating. When you understand why you have become involved with an emotionally abusive person and why you have allowed someone to continually abuse you, you will begin to feel less critical of yourself and be better able to stop the abuse.

To break your negative patterns, you will need to work on completing the unfinished business of your past. This will be the focus of the next chapter.

CHAPTER 5

Completing Your Unfinished Business

By allowing yourself to continue to be abused in the same ways you were as a child, you are deepening the wounds from your childhood and avoiding your real work—completing your unfinished business. Unfinished business can include any or all of the following: feelings you haven't expressed, things you have left unsaid, false hopes you are still holding on to, and conflicts left unresolved.

Aside from continually being involved with abusive people, a sign that you have unfinished business with your parents or other abusers is the amount of time you spend thinking about the past. Do you think about the abuse a great deal of the time? Do you obsess about your parents or other abusers? Do you ruminate about what you would like to say to them, what you would like to do to them? Are you continually thinking vengeful thoughts, planning ways of getting back at them, of hurting them? Obsessive thinking is a sign th ' you are avoiding something or hiding something from yourself (usually, your true feelings), and it is also a way of avoiding confronting your original abuser.

The need to continually repeat the past is a very compelling and unconscious drive. Unless you complete your unfinished business, you are destined to continue this pattern, becoming involved time after time with the same kind of abusive person and situation.

If you were my client, I would begin by having you recount how you were emotionally abused as a child and encourage you to allow yourself to feel the emotions of shame, anger, sadness, and fear that this abuse created in you. If you were to have a difficult time reconnecting with your emotions and memories of the past, I might have you work on connecting with your inner child. This technique has helped many people to remember the past and gain access to their emotions. I would also encourage you to feel your anger toward your original abuser, and to release this anger in a constructive way. Anger empowers us and helps us to put the responsibility for the abuse where it belongs instead of on ourselves. I would encourage you to mourn your childhood and let go of the false hope of ever getting from your parents what you didn't get as a child.

The entire healing process would likely take quite some time. During this time, you would be working on becoming more self-reliant, learning to trust your own judgment and perceptions, and raising your self-esteem.

While working on healing the past, you might feel pressured to decide whether to leave your current abusive relationship. This pressure might come from inside you, or it might come from well-meaning friends and family. Ideally, in working toward healing you would decide on your own either that you were strong enough to stand up to your current abuser and refuse to allow him to continue to mistreat you, or that you no longer wanted or needed to be involved in a relationship that was just a carbon copy of your relationship with your original abuser.

There simply isn't enough space for me to tell you here all that you need to know in order to heal from your past abuse and to complete your unfinished business. But even if I were to try, I would be doing you a disservice to imply that you can do this kind of intensive, deeply unsettling work on your own. You will need the support and guidance of a qualified, licensed psychotherapist. Depending upon the kind of emotional abuse you suffered as a child, you may need extensive work with a specially trained professional. Or, you may need therapy for only a short period of time and be able to get continued support from a group such as Adult Children of Alcoholics or Codependents Anonymous.

I do, however, have a caveat to offer with regard to group settings: while those who have suffered physical and sexual abuse may gain a great deal from self-help groups, group therapy, or

Twelve-Step programs, those who have been emotionally abused (especially if that abuse has involved severe neglect and constant criticism) may not benefit as much from such groups. Group therapy can feel like torture to people who have suffered severe criticism, since they may assume that others are critical of them even when they are not. They may be so afraid of saying the "wrong thing" that they are unable to speak up in a group. Similarly, those who have been severely neglected may find it unbearable to have to share the attention of the group leader. This type of situation may remind them of the deprivation of their childhood, when they were ignored by a parent.

I strongly recommend at least short-term individual therapy for women who were emotionally abused as children and who continue to be emotionally abused as adults. Only on a one-to-one basis can you begin to work through the issues of trust, intimacy, and bonding, gain a stronger sense of self, and learn to be separate from someone you are close to. Only by establishing a caring and trusting relationship with a supportive person who has firm and clear boundaries can you work through your fears of betrayal, criticism, abandonment, and suffocation. You will then be ready to move on to supportive group sessions, if you choose to do so.

The issues outlined in this chapter for completing your unfinished business are some of the major issues you will need to address in therapy. If you do not feel ready to enter therapy yet, you can still start the healing process by beginning to focus on these issues now.

In working to complete your unfinished business, you will:

☐ discover what your unfinished business is

☐ reclaim your buried emotions from the past

☐ release your anger and confront your original abuser

☐ resolve your relationship with your original abuser

☐ separate emotionally from your parents

☐ let go of the false hope of ever getting what you didn't get as a child

☐ become your own good parent

DISCOVERING YOUR UNFINISHED BUSINESS

Discovering exactly what your unfinished business is will be an ongoing process. The following exercise can help you discover where to begin:

1. Answer the following questions: What is your relationship with your original abuser now? Do you ever see him? Are you close? Do you still feel abused by him?
2. List all the reasons you are still angry with your *original* abuser. List all the reasons you are still hurt.
3. Make a list of what you want from your original abuser now.
4. List the reasons you feel angry with and hurt by your *current* abuser.
5. Make a list of what you want from your current abuser.
6. Compare the lists from #2 and #4. Then compare the lists from #3 and #5.

This is what June discovered from the above exercise:

I realized that I still feel very angry at my father and hurt by him, even though I haven't seen him in eight years. I thought I was finished with him—that he had no impact on my life at this time—but now I know that isn't true. Just thinking about how he treated me as a child still makes me feel terrible. Although I tried not to think about the abuse or about him for years, I recognize now that the feelings are still there. I also realized that I am hurt and angry with my husband for essentially the same reasons. I even wanted them both to do the same things: stop drinking, stop criticizing me, and stop blaming me for all their problems. I married a man who is so much like my father it's ridiculous.

I realize that I have been acting out toward my husband the feelings I have for my father. While it's true that my husband also hurts and angers me, by far the deeper pain and anger involves my father. I know now that I have to release my feelings about my father before I can be clear about what I want to do about my relationship with my husband. I need to separate the two relationships, because right now they're both mixed up together in my mind.

Reclaiming Your Emotions

A great part of the damage caused by childhood abuse of any kind is that it causes us to disown our emotions, to push them down until we are no longer aware of them or have lost control of them. We may then enter a state of emotional bankruptcy, "sleepwalking" through life and depriving ourselves (and others) of any emotionality. Or, we may become emotional volcanoes, spewing out our pain and anger at anyone in our path, erupting without a moment's notice and causing upset after upset.

Allow Yourself to Express Your Feelings

As victims of childhood abuse, we typically have a difficult time expressing our feelings. In part, this is simply because we are not used to doing so: we are more accustomed to repressing our emotions, ignoring or minimizing our pain, and hiding how we really feel from ourselves and from others. We often become frightened whenever we feel anything intensely, whether it be anger, fear, pain, or even love and joy. We are afraid that our feelings will overpower us, make us crazy. We imagine our emotions spilling out all over the place, creating havoc in our lives.

In reality, it is what we *don't* express that can get us into trouble. The more we repress our feelings, the more likely it is that they will burst out when we least expect it. You will not "go crazy" if you allow yourself to feel and express your strong emotions. If you consistently allow yourself to express your feelings when they occur instead of holding them in, you will find that you will actually feel *more* in control of your emotions, not less. As one of my clients told me,

> I was afraid that once I started allowing my feelings to surface I wouldn't have any control. I had held them in for so long, I was sure they would just burst out and I'd be like a crazy person! But you know what? I just started letting them out a little at a time, and I was okay!

Why Are We So Accustomed to Denying Our Feelings?

We learned at an early age that expressing emotions is a negative thing and that we should suppress and deny our feelings. Often, one or both of our parents were very cut off from their feelings and were thus nonexpressive and nonaffectionate. As children, we were likely told that we were "too sensitive" or "felt too strongly about things." We were told that we overreacted to situations, making too much of things. However, chances are that we were actually reacting normally. Our parents probably felt threatened by our reactions, since they tended to avoid their own feelings.

We may have learned to deny our feelings because we lived in a home where we were taught to ignore the reality of how bad things really were. Time after time we were told that something had not happened, even though we knew it had. Janine shared with me her experience as a child:

> My parents would have these horrible fights. They would keep us awake half the night with their screaming. The next morning my mother's face would be bruised and battered, and she would tell everyone that she had run into a door.

Another client, Celeste, told me how she learned to deny reality:

> My mother had what everyone called "spells." She would go around the house muttering to herself, seeming to see right through me, as if I weren't there. She would dress up in weird outfits and dance by herself to imaginary music. Then she would break out into these bloodcurdling screams, start crying hysterically, and lock herself up in her room for days at a time. Our entire family denied that she needed psychiatric help, even though she had episode after episode of this insane behavior.

With all this denial going on, it's no wonder that we grew up not being able to trust our own feelings or perceptions.

Another reason for our tendency to deny and avoid feelings is that we often had to disconnect from our emotions as a method of survival during times of chaos or abuse. The emotional and/or physical trauma we suffered during abuse was often so severe that our bodies had to "shut down" to protect us from such a deluge of pain. All of our senses were dulled. Some victims have reported that they consciously induced numbness in parts of their bodies. Others experienced a form of "losing consciousness," dissociating themselves from their bodies and from their feelings.

As adults, many of us still function as if in a daze, just going through the motions of being alive. We became so good at dissociating ourselves from life in order to avoid pain that we are seldom truly present when we are with other people (since we are seldom comfortable with people). Generally, we are daydreaming about something else or obsessing about what we have to do next; rarely do we fully experience the moment.

We are, in fact, so afraid of pain that we deny its existence. We feel proud of our ability to tolerate painful situations, when what we are actually doing is numbing ourselves. We even pride ourselves on our ability to quietly withstand even extreme physical pain, seeing it as a sign of strength. We foolishly think that it's best to ignore pain of any kind in the hope that it will just go away. By splitting ourselves off from our physical and emotional feelings, we may, indeed, manage to avoid a good deal of pain—but the price we pay is that we are never fully alive. We are now cut off from *all* of our feelings, good as well as bad.

Our state of slumber has become a nightmare, and our real self is hidden from us. In order to recover, we must integrate our bodies with our minds and our emotions with our thoughts.

Kelly, a drama junkie, began to get in touch with one of the reasons she is so addicted to chaos:

> In my family, there was so much chaos and trauma going on all the time that I just numbed out. I just couldn't tolerate all the yelling, all the fighting, and all the violence, so I would just kind of "go away" in my mind. I guess I did this so I wouldn't go crazy. Now, though, I notice that a lot of the time I still don't feel very much. I think I create chaos in my life just so I can feel *something*.

The most effective way to reclaim all of your emotions (pain, anger, fear, guilt, shame, joy, and love) is to begin to pay attention to your body. Even when we unconsciously repress our feelings, our bodies still remember them. These memories are called *body memories*. Your body holds memories of what it was like when you were a child, how it felt when you were neglected, criticized, and rejected. It remembers the pain and anger with stiffness, constrictions, and tension. For each emotion, your body experiences a different set of physical sensations. As you continue to bring back memories of your childhood, your body will react naturally. Heed your body's messages, and allow the natural physical reactions to occur.

RELEASING YOUR ANGER AND CONFRONTING YOUR ORIGINAL ABUSER

Resentment is the most frequent kind of unfinished business. It is natural and normal for you to feel resentment (which translates into anger) toward your original abusers for doing any or all of the following:

☐ emotionally abusing you

☐ physically or sexually abusing you

☐ damaging your self-esteem

☐ being poor role models

☐ setting you up to be a victim

☐ setting you up to be attracted to abusive people

☐ not teaching you how to take care of yourself

☐ not acknowledging to you that they abused you as a child

If you are still angry with one or more of your original abusers, you need to ventilate this anger. When we remain angry with others, we stay emotionally tied to them in a very negative way. We continue to feel victimized by them, and we continue to invest a tremendous amount of energy in them by focusing on and blaming them. Carrying the burden of anger and hatred around causes us to feel a great deal of tension and anxiety. Unexpressed anger gets turned inward on ourselves, making us feel guilty, inadequate, and worthless.

While anger is a natural, healthy emotion when ventilated properly, blame is a wasted and negative experience. You are angry with your original abusers because they deprived, controlled, and criticized you. This doesn't mean that you blame them, but that you hold them accountable for their behavior. The difference between anger and blame is that blaming keeps you caught up in the problem, while releasing your anger constructively allows you to work through the problem. Continually blaming others for what they have done to us in the past keeps us stuck in the past, and we remain emotional children. When we release our anger, in healthful ways toward those who abused and damaged us, we are able to step out of blame and let go of the past.

No one can "stand in" for your original abuser. No matter how often you get angry at your current abuser, it doesn't satisfy your need to get angry at the original one.

However, releasing your anger toward your original abuser can empower you to also stand up to your present abusers, tell them that you are not going to take it anymore, and *mean* it. In so doing, you can free yourself of the past, release yourself from a painful present, and plant the seeds for a healthier tomorrow.

Giving Yourself Permission to Be Angry

It is sometimes difficult to get past our prior conditioning about anger. Our society does not give women permission to express anger. We are given much more permission to cry than we are to express righteous anger or to assert ourselves. Those women who do dare to express their anger are seen as being out of control. For these reasons it will take courage to admit that you are angry and to face the person you are angry with, either directly or indirectly. It will take courage to be honest about your anger, because by doing so you are also acknowledging that you are hurt. It takes no courage to push the anger down and to pretend that you don't care. That is the "safe" but unhealthy way out.

Gena came into therapy because she had once again gotten involved with an extremely abusive man. An intensely shy, apologetic, and self-effacing person, she repeatedly said throughout our sessions, "I'm sorry, I don't know what's wrong with me. I shouldn't be taking up your time." In essence, Gena was "sorry" for existing! Her guilt was so overwhelming that she often felt like committing suicide.

As Gena revealed her story, it became clear that aside from food and shelter, Gena's mother had given her none of the things a child needs: nurturing, protection, attention, instruction, or encouragement. When I asked Gena if she was angry with her mother for having deprived her, she said, "No, why should I be angry? I don't blame my mother—I was a terrible kid. My mother couldn't stand to be around me, and I don't blame her." When I asked Gena where she got the idea that she was a terrible kid, she said, "My mother told me I was. And why else would she have ignored me like that?"

Gena saw that the fact that most of her friends, bosses, and lovers had treated her poorly as further evidence that she was a bad person. It never occurred to her that she chose friends and lovers who were like her mother, or that because of her tremendous guilt she allowed others to abuse her.

For Gena, the hardest and most important part of recovery was finally admitting her anger toward her mother and learning how to release it in nonthreatening ways. Because she had been physically abused, she was afraid of any physical display of anger. She was, however, able to write down her angry feelings toward her mother. The more she did this, the more in touch with reality she became. Memories and images of her childhood began to come back, reminding her of how abusive her mother had really been.

The more Gena released her anger, the less guilty she felt. Slowly, she became less apologetic and less self-effacing. This was three and a half years ago. Today, Gena no longer feels guilty and thus no longer has the need to get involved in abusive relationships. She no longer has suicidal thoughts. For the first time, she feels like planning her future, and she is enrolling in law school in the fall. Although she still suffers some negative effects from her devastating childhood, Gena continues to work in therapy on learning ways of providing for herself what she wasn't given as a child.

In addition to alleviating guilt, shame, and self-hatred, releasing your anger toward your original abuser will:

☐ Improve your self-esteem. When you stop blaming yourself and no longer turn your anger inward, you will begin to feel better about yourself.

☐ Make you feel lighter, raise your spirits, and give you hope. You will feel as if a tremendous burden has been lifted from your shoulders.

☐ Release physical tension. When you suppress your anger, you hold your body rigid so that your feelings cannot escape. When you release your anger, your body becomes more relaxed, more mobile.

☐ Free you to express love and joy and experience feelings of pleasure.

☐ Clarify your thinking and improve your decision-making abilities. Your thinking will become less confused when you are less distracted by your anger.

☐ Help you feel your emotional strength, physical strength, and personal power. Releasing your anger will help to empower you. It will help you to be less afraid of others and better able to stand up for yourself and to be more assertive.

☐ Help you become an independent person, enabling you to mentally and emotionally separate from your parents and leave destructive relationships.

☐ Improve your relationships, since you will no longer be so likely to choose abusive people or to take your anger out on your mate, children, friends, and coworkers.

☐ Help you to become a survivor, reducing the feelings of hopelessness and helplessness that keep you a victim.

☐ Help you to let go of past hurts.

☐ Help you to forgive yourself and others.

☐ Give you the courage to change.

If you release your anger in an honest, direct, constructive way, it will dissipate. Releasing your anger will not change what has happened or change the other person, but it will change *you*.

The Confrontation: Releasing Your Anger in Positive Ways

How do you go about ventilating your anger toward your original abuser? There are many effective ways of constructively releasing your anger. If you feel that a direct confrontation would be fruitful for you, by all means do so, if you can do it without endangering yourself. However, you need not directly confront the abuser. Your original abuser may be dead, or he may be too old or too sick to handle a direct confrontation. Or he may still be so abusive, unreasonable, threatening, or crazy that you do not wish to risk your safety and emotional well-being by confronting him directly. You may even have already tried dealing with him directly, to no avail. All of the suggestions that follow can be applied to both direct and indirect confrontations.

LETTER-WRITING.   One of the most beneficial ways of releasing anger is to write your original abuser a letter that you do not send. Write down everything you have always wanted to say, making sure that you include the follow points:

☐ what the abuser did to anger/hurt you

☐ how it damaged you and influenced your life

☐ how you feel about him now

Don't ask questions, such as "How could you . . . ?" or "Why did you . . . ?" Questions help maintain your role as victim. Instead, make *statements,* beginning with "I," such as "I'm angry with you for . . . " or "I don't like what you did when . . . " Be assertive. When you are done, you may tear up the letter, keep it, or even mail it, if you choose.

IMAGINARY CONVERSATIONS.   You may also wish to have an imaginary conversation with your abuser. Pretend you are talking to your original abuser, and tell this person exactly how you feel. Say everything you have ever wanted to say. Don't hold anything back. You might pretend the person you are angry with is sitting in a chair across from you (it may help to put a picture of the person on the chair). Or, you might wish to express your feelings of anger into a tape recorder, speaking as though you were talking directly to your abuser.

RELEASING THE ANGER PHYSICALLY.   Because your body is storing the anger, it can be especially helpful for you to release your anger physically. Ask yourself, "What does my body usually feel like doing when I am angry? Does it feel like kicking, hitting, throwing things, or screaming?" If you feel like hitting, for example, it is because you have been holding your anger in the parts of the body that are involved with hitting—your shoulders, neck, arms, hands, and back. (Please note: if you answered "My body feels like crying," be aware that crying is *not* an adequate way of releasing *anger*. Crying is the way to express pain and sadness. Victims in general and women in particular often cry when they are really feeling angry. It is socially more acceptable for a woman to cry than to express anger. Also, when you were a child your parents may have allowed you to cry but punished you if you showed anger.)

Start out slowly if you wish, but do a little "anger release" work each day. Pick up a newspaper or magazine, roll it up, and smack your kitchen table or couch each time you come into the room. Walk around your house growling like a dog, making faces, or grunting. Punch the air like a boxer, kick large pillows, or stomp on aluminum cans. The important thing is that you make releasing your anger an integral part of your life. Make it as important as anything else you do for your health.

Confronting Your Abuser

FANTASY CONFRONTATION.   Confronting your original abuser, even if it is an indirect confrontation, will enable you to take back your power and prove to yourself that you are no longer going to allow him to frighten or control you. By facing your abuser with the truth and your feelings no matter how frightened you are, you are breaking into the cycle of victimization and are no longer being impotent, passive, and ineffectual, allowing things to happen to you.

You can use the following visualization exercise either as an indirect way of confronting or as a practice confrontation to prepare you for an actual encounter.

1. Lie down or sit in a comfortable position with pillows under your hands. Close your eyes, breathe deeply, and relax.
2. Decide who you are going to confront, and visualize this person.
3. Visualize a safe place where you can have your confrontation. You may choose your own home, a public place, or perhaps somewhere outside where there would be plenty of space so you could get away easily.
4. You are going to be in the unique position of being able to see your abuser before he sees you. Notice his facial expression and posture as he is approaching you. Notice any changes in these things after he has noticed you.
5. Sit down facing each other and begin your confrontation. You are going to speak first, and he is not going to be able to interrupt you or speak until you are finished. Try to speak out loud if you can, or just imagine what you would say. Breathe deeply throughout the exercise.
6. After you have said all that you want to say, rest quietly for a few minutes. Cry if you need to. If you wish, allow the other person to have a turn to speak. What do you imagine his response would be to what you have said?
7. Now it is your turn again. Respond to what the abuser has said to you.
8. If you are angered by the response, or if you don't agree with something that has been said, quietly begin saying no. Continue saying no, louder and louder each time. Yell "NO!" at each exhale of your breath, remembering to breathe deeply.
9. If you have built up a lot of anger and need to release it physically, begin to hit the pillows with your fists. With each exhale, come down hard with your fists onto the pillows and yell "NO!"
10. Allow any feelings or tears to come while you rest from the confrontation. When you get up, write down your experience if you choose. You may also want to share the experience with a supportive friend.

DIRECT CONFRONTATION.   If you choose to confront your original abuser directly, practice your confrontation by writing it down, speaking into a tape recorder, or talking out loud first. You can practice by yourself, with a friend, or with a therapist. The following format provides a guide or script.

1. List what your abuser did to make you feel angry, hurt, damaged, guilty, ashamed, and afraid. State each abuse, injustice, injury, damage, and painful memory you have.

   Examples:

   You neglected me terribly.

   You criticized me constantly, making me feel as though I could never do anything right.

   You competed with me, always trying to prove that you could do anything better than I could.

   You tried to control me completely, never letting me make a decision on my own.

2. List how you felt as a result of the abuser's behavior.

   Examples:

   I felt unloved and unworthy of being loved.

   I felt extremely inadequate and believed that there was something wrong with me.

   I felt extremely angry with you for not acting like an adult.

   I felt totally helpless to break out of the prison of your control.

3. List what effects your abuser's actions (or inactions) have had on you, and how your life has been affected. Include both childhood effects and repercussions you experience as an adult.

   Examples:

   As a child:

   It caused me to have very low self-esteem.

   It caused me to become very self-critical.

I knew I could never measure up to you, so I just stopped trying.

Other children saw me as a wimp who they could control.

As an adult:

It has caused me to be self-destructive.

It has destroyed my feelings of self-worth.

I am extremely fearful of competition. If someone does better than I, I just give up.

I let other people control me just like you did.

4. Tell him how you feel about him *now,* and why.

Examples:

I feel afraid you will let me down again.

I feel angry with you for damaging my life.

I feel ashamed of you for always having to compete with me.

I love you, but I am afraid you will try to control me again.

5. List everything you want from him *now.*

Examples:

I want you to listen to me when I talk, ask questions about my life, and not monopolize all our conversations.

I want you to treat me with respect and consideration and not criticize me anymore.

I want you to stop competing with me, and I want you to act like a mother instead of a jealous sister.

I want you to recognize that I am an adult, and I want you to stop trying to control me.

Before you confront your abuser directly, you will need to make the following preparations:

1. Take the edge off your anger by using any number of anger-releasing techniques (hitting a pillow or screaming into it).

2. Rehearse your confrontation until you are sure of what you want to say.

3. Just as you did in the fantasy confrontation, prepare yourself by deciding when and where you would feel most comfortable and secure having the confrontation. Many people prefer to have the confrontation take place in the therapist's office. If you are apprehensive about violence, rage, or loss of control—even if it is your own—you may need to have a third party present.

4. Set some ground rules for the confrontation, and determine how you will express them to your abuser. Here are some examples:

   I want you to hear me out before you respond.

   I don't want you to interrupt me or stop me.

   I don't want you to defend, justify, or rationalize.

5. Obtain a commitment to the ground rules from your abuser *before* you proceed. If your abuser is unwilling to do even this much, it is probably better to try the confrontation at a later date. Remember, you have the advantage. You have decided when, where, and under what circumstances the confrontation will take place. You are prepared; the abuser is not.

6. Even if your abuser agrees not to interrupt, be prepared for a counterattack both during and after your confrontation. If he interrupts you too often, tell him that you are going to leave (or will ask him to leave) if he doesn't keep his commitment. Expect the worst, including any of the following responses:

   ☐ Denial ("You're lying," "You're exaggerating," "I don't remember," "That never happened")

   ☐ Blame ("You were such a difficult child," "You're crazy," "I had to do something to control you")

   ☐ Rationalizations ("I did the best I could," "Things were really tough," "I tried to stop drinking, but I couldn't")

   ☐ Self-pity ("I have enough problems without this," "How could you do this to me?")

   ☐ Guilt ("Look what we did for you," "Nothing was ever enough for you," "This is the thanks I get")

Don't buy into any of this. Just stick with what you want to say until you are completely finished.
7. Make sure you have supportive people to talk to before and after your confrontation.
8. Be prepared to end the confrontation whenever you decide its effectiveness is over because you feel threatened, you feel you or the abuser is losing control, your abuser is too busy defending himself to really hear you, or it has turned into a shouting match.

No matter how clear, reasonable, or articulate you are in your confrontation or in your responses to counterattacks, some abusers will twist your words and your motives. They will accuse, lie, and generally make you feel as though you are crazy. Keep in mind, however, that sometimes confrontations that end in anger may eventually lead to positive changes once the initial uproar is over. Give your abuser some time to think about what you have said before you assume he or she didn't hear you or take what you said seriously.

RESOLVING YOUR RELATIONSHIP WITH YOUR ORIGINAL ABUSER

After you have released your anger toward your original abuser and completed either an indirect or direct confrontation, you will need to resolve your relationship with him or her so that you can go on with your life. This is particularly true when your original abuser is a family member.

If your abuser has shown some capacity for understanding your pain and some willingness to take responsibility for his actions—however small this capacity and willingness may seem—there may be hope for the relationship. If he is willing to continue discussing the conflicts between you, you may be able to teach him what does and what does not feel good to you in the relationship.

If your abuser is willing to listen to you, to accept responsibility for his actions, and to apologize to you, you may feel like forgiving him. Forgiving doesn't mean that you forget or ignore the past, but that you recognize that it's possible for a person to change and begin again. If you are able to forgive, you'll feel a sense of relief and a new freedom within yourself.

On the other hand, you may discover that your abuser is not open to looking at what he has done to damage you. Your parents or other original abusers may continue to abuse you in the same ways they always have. They may be unwilling or unable to establish a positive relationship with you. If this is the case, you may need to temporarily separate from them or even "divorce" them.

Marnie divorced both her mother and her father. Her father is a very emotionally abusive man and had berated Marnie from the time she was a little girl, telling her she was stupid, ugly, and good for nothing. He would fly into uncontrollable rages for little or no reason, and afterward he would send Marnie and her siblings to their rooms. Marnie's mother was essentially unavailable to her children. She was aloof, preoccupied, and emotionally empty, providing her children absolutely no protection from their raving, ranting father.

Not surprisingly, Marnie suffered from extremely low self-esteem and a feeling of worthlessness. It took her many years of therapy to even begin to believe that she could support herself emotionally and financially and that she was a worthwhile human being. Two years ago, Marnie divorced her father because he was unwilling to admit that he had sexually abused her when she was a very little girl. In addition, she divorced her mother because her mother refused to believe that Marnie's father could have done such a thing, and also because she felt that her mother had essentially taken her father's side and wasn't being supportive to her. In addition, she recognized how much her father was still controlling her mother, even though they had been divorced for several years. Recognizing just how deeply disturbed both her parents were, Marnie realized she needed to break away from them to save her own sanity.

Marnie's story is typical among people from dysfunctional homes. Before you take such drastic action, however, discuss the pros and cons of such a decision with your therapist. In addition, you may wish to read my book *Divorcing a Parent*.

SEPARATING EMOTIONALLY FROM YOUR PARENTS

If one or both of your parents were your original abusers, it's time to develop your own identity and become your own person, with your own values, beliefs, priorities, and opinions. While you will always be influenced by your parents, you need to make your own way, not just follow theirs.

If you do not go through a process of emotionally separating from your parents, you will not be able to choose which things about them you want to identify with. Instead, you will identify with the totality of them, and you may end up being just like them. If you see that you have a tendency to be like one of your parents in a particular way that you don't like (such as being passive and allowing others to abuse you), you will need to take a stand against that way of being in order to be truly different from your parent. One of the many benefits of releasing your anger toward your original abuser is that getting angry does help you to separate from, and take a stand against, the abuser.

Separation is a natural process of becoming a psychologically separate human being and developing your own unique personality. This process evolves slowly, over time. If you are in therapy, you are already in the process, since therapy helps you become strong enough to emotionally separate from your parents. You do not necessarily need to understand the process; it happens naturally and spontaneously.

Those who were abused as children seldom have a strong sense of themselves. You cannot separate completely and stand alone until you have established a sense of "selfness," a sense of who you are. This core of self cannot be taken away. Our sense of identity depends partly on our knowledge that our true self endures over time, despite changes around us. (In chapter 8, we will discuss ways of discovering your self.)

An important aspect of separating from your parents is learning the differences between you and them. To explore these differences, make a list of the characteristics of each of your parents (and/or of another primary caretaker, if appropriate), then a list of your own. Include both positive and negative characteristics on each list.

My mother is (was):

Example: Frightened
        Insecure
        Aloof

_____

_____

My father is (was):

Example: Angry
        Moody
        Stubborn

_____

_____

My (other primary caretaker) is (was):

Example:
My grandmother was: Loving
                    Generous
                    Kind

_____

_____

I am:

Example: Insecure
        Angry
        Sensitive

_____

_____

In looking at the lists you have made, you will more than likely find that you share some characteristics of the people who reared you. You also have qualities that are unique to you. You can remain like your parents in positive ways, but you can choose not to follow in their footsteps completely and make the same mistakes they made. You can thus develop a balance of behaviors and attitudes that feel right for *you.*

Sometimes our lives are dictated by our attempts to *not* be like one of our parents. Unfortunately, your only other significant role model may have been the other parent, who instead of being healthy simply had a different set of problems.

Lynn, for example, decided early on that she was never going to be like her abusive father.

> My father was a monster! He had this horribly violent temper, and he would periodically "go off" at my mother or me. My mother, on the other hand, was so passive that she would never stand up to anyone. She still lets my father abuse her and never says a thing. I decided a long time ago that I wasn't going to be like him. But instead, I've turned out to be as passive as my mother.

If you notice behavior in yourself that you do not like, ask yourself, "Am I behaving this way because I don't want to be like my parent?" or "Am I acting like one parent as some kind of guarantee that I won't be like the other parent?"

Melissa's parents were extremely rigid and strict with her. Everything she did had to be done in just a certain way, or she would be punished and have to do it over. Her room had to be immaculate, her clothes had to be pressed perfectly, her school papers could not have any erasures. As an adult, Melissa is extremely disorganized and undisciplined—the opposite of her parents.

> I want to have more control over my life, but every time I start to get organized I become afraid I am becoming like my parents. I hate my life the way it is, but I just can't risk ending up like them, so I just stay the way I am and hate myself for it.

By focusing all her attention on making sure she was not like her parents, Melissa had not discovered *herself.*

LETTING GO OF FALSE HOPE

A major part of resolving your relationship with your original abusers will be letting go of any false hope that you will ever get from them what you didn't get as a child, or that you can undo what has already been done. You will need to mourn the loss of your childhood and acknowledge that your parents will never be the loving, supportive parents you have always wanted them to be.

You will also need to acknowledge that no one is going to come along and bestow on you what you so longed to get from your parents. It is now up to you to begin to nurture yourself.

Paige always got involved with men who treated her like a child. Her own father had emotionally abandoned her when she was a child, rejecting her attempts to be close and refusing to spend time with her. Unconsciously, Paige was still looking for the good father she had never had. Generally, she chose men who were older and more worldly than she. Unfortunately, these men were not all "good daddies." Many of them insisted on being in control of the relationship and of how Paige ran her life. Although she wanted to be taken care of, Paige did not want to be controlled. She needed to learn that getting involved with surrogate "daddies" was keeping her a child, and that she was never going to get the fathering she had missed out on.

In her book *Necessary Losses,* Judith Viorst writes about our repetition compulsion:

> For we cannot climb into a time machine, become that long-gone child and get what we want when we oh so desperately wanted it. The days for that getting are over, finished, done. We have needs we can meet in different ways, in better ways, in ways that create new experiences. But until we can mourn the past, until we can mourn and let go of the past, we are doomed to repeat it.

You must mourn the loss of your childhood, the loss of your "fantasy" parents, and the loss of your false hope that you can ever get now what you didn't get then.

BECOMING YOUR OWN GOOD PARENT

Although you cannot expect anyone else to give to you what you were deprived of as a child, you can begin to provide these things for yourself. Becoming your own good parent, giving yourself the nurturing and caring that you are still so much in need of, is an important part of completing your unfinished business. Once you begin to be your own good parent, you will be less resentful of those in your childhood who deprived and neglected you. To let go of the past and understand fully that you must stop yearning for something that will never be, you must become your own good parent.

Although you may not remember your early childhood feelings, you have unknowingly incorporated into yourself the child you once were, with her fears and insecurities and her desperate need to be loved. That child is as alive and with you, as forceful a presence, as if she were living in your household.

According to many experts, your inner child is the symbolic representation of all your past and present emotions. Many of your current beliefs and emotions actually come from your inner child. For example, the belief that you have to be good all the time to be loved comes from the child within you, who is still looking for what you wanted so desperately when you were little.

Discovering the Child Within

The following exercise will help you to identify your inner child:

1. Lie down or sit in a comfortable position.
2. Close your eyes and start doing some deep breathing, inhaling as much air as possible and then expelling all the air before taking another deep breath. Do this for a minute or two, or until you feel relaxed.
3. With your eyes still closed, visualize your inner child as you imagine she would look.
4. Notice how you feel about her. Do you like her?
5. Notice how she seems to feel about you. Does she seem open to you, or does she seem rejecting?

6. Try to make some contact with her, whether it be touching her hand, hugging her, or just making eye contact with her. How does she react? Does she welcome contact with you, or does she turn away?

If you are having a difficult time visualizing your inner child, try the following exercise:

1. Look through old family albums until you find some pictures of yourself when you were a child. Pick out a picture of yourself as an infant, as a toddler, as a young child, and as an adolescent. Choose pictures that most remind you of how you remember feeling at these particular ages.
2. Study each picture carefully for several minutes, and then see if you can retain the image of it when you close your eyes. If you cannot do so, just try it again. Continue until you can see the image of yourself as an infant, a toddler, a young child, and an adolescent at will.

Now go back to the visualization exercise and try it again, using the memories of the photos as reminders of how you looked.

Once you have identified your inner child, you can begin to communicate with her, finding out how she feels and what she needs and reassuring her that you are there for her. This can be a verbal or written dialogue, an imaginary conversation between the adult part of you and the child part of you. Start your dialogue with a question such as "How are you today?" or "Is something bothering you? You seem upset." With practice, your inner child will express what she is feeling. The adult in you will then be able to listen to the child, soothe her, and assume responsibility for her—in essence, becoming the good parent you never had. While as a child you were truly helpless, unable to stop someone from being abusive to you, as an adult you can stand up not only for yourself but also for the child within you.

Many discover that their inner child is reluctant to trust them. Your inner child needs to learn to trust that you will protect and nurture her, not neglect and abuse her as the other adults in her life have done. In time, you can establish a good relationship with your inner child. If you continually work on connecting with her, you will be surprised how real her voice will become and how much you will grow to depend on her to tell you what is going on with you.

Reassuring Your Inner Child

Who you are today is greatly determined by what you learned or did not learn as a child. As a child, at each phase of the process of separating from your parents you grew, got stuck, or regressed. When emotional, physical, or sexual abuse occurs, children often regress in their development and revert back to a very primary developmental stage in order to survive. They may then be unable to progress in their development as they should. However, if you give yourself the security, comfort, and nurturing you missed as a child, you do not have to allow any impairments in your early development to interfere with your life today or with your ability to become an independent self.

Be loving to yourself. Give yourself strokes, encouragement, and acknowledgment. Give yourself a lot of positive self-talk. For example: "You did well," "I know how hard that was for you—at least you tried," "You're a wonderful girl," "You'll be okay—I'll take care of you," and "I love you."

Perhaps the strongest reason we have for maintaining a relationship with our parents, however destructive that relationship may be, is our intense fear that without them we will be all alone in a cold world. Since the child inside does not know that she can survive without these parents, she will at first feel totally abandoned, helpless, and alone at the thought of separating from them. Therefore, it will be absolutely necessary for you to reassure her that she will not be alone but will have you to care for her. The following exercise will help you to reassure your inner child:

☐ Lying in a comfortable position, imagine you are holding your inner child. You can hold a stuffed animal or a pillow, if you wish. First in your imagination and then out loud, start saying, "I will protect you. I will never allow any harm to come to you. I will never allow anyone to abuse you or humiliate you." Say it over and over, until your inner child hears you. Repeat this exercise at least once a week.

Just as a new mother begins to feel more and more confident as she realizes she is doing a good job with her new baby, so you will gain courage, strength, and confidence as you continue to reach out to your inner child and take good care of her.

Completing your unfinished business will take a lot of time and effort, but you will find that there is nothing more worthwhile than working to set yourself free of the past. While the emotional abuse you suffered as a child will never be washed away completely, by releasing your pain and anger from the past, confronting those who hurt you either directly or indirectly, and becoming your own good parent, you will be giving yourself the gift of a life in which you can freely choose who you want to be and who you want in your life.

As you complete your unfinished business, you may also be deciding whether to leave your current abusive relationship or whether to stay. In the next two chapters, we will discuss both of these options in detail.

PART
3

DECIDING WHAT
TO DO NEXT

CHAPTER 6

Should You Stay, or Should You Leave?

Realizing that your current abuser is a replica of your original abuser can help set you free. You will either decide to leave because staying in your current relationship would be like being abused all over again by your original abuser, or you will decide to stay because you feel you are now able to stop buying into the abuser's blaming and to defend yourself. Ali told me why she decided to leave her boyfriend:

> Once I saw that my boyfriend was just like my father, I realized how hopeless the relationship really was. I remembered all the years I had spent trying to get my father to change and to make him love me, all to no avail. I realized that I had picked someone just like him, and that I was doing the same thing—trying to make someone love me who is basically incapable of loving. I knew then that I needed to get out.

Kitty, having realized that she had married a man like her original abuser, felt the opposite—that now she could stay and have a healthier relationship:

> Once I realized that I had chosen someone just like my mother, I recognized that my husband wasn't going to change any more than my mother had, and that he wasn't going to make up for what my mother hadn't done for me. After this, I began to appreciate him for himself.

If you are involved with someone who emotionally abuses you in the same ways you were abused as a child, each time you allow this person to abuse you, you are exacerbating the damage you experienced as a child. Because of this, you may be feeling that the decision of whether to stay or leave is your most pressing issue at this time.

WHEN IS IT BEST TO LEAVE?

If you have identified your current abuser as an antisocial personality, a misogynist, a narcissist, or a destroyer, there is little hope for the relationship. Such people have serious emotional disturbances and require intensive, long-term psychotherapy if there is to be any hope for change. No matter how much they want to change, or how hard they try, they simply can't do it on their own.

Although I run the risk of oversimplifying, if any of the following circumstances exist in your current relationship *in general,* it is probably best that you begin working on leaving the relationship:

1. YOUR PARTNER IS NOW, OR IS THREATENING TO BECOME, PHYSICALLY VIOLENT.
Physical abusers often begin by emotionally abusing their victims. The more emotional abuse a woman takes, the more permission the abuser feels he has to be abusive. As his anger intensifies and as the relationship deteriorates, he may resort to physical violence as a way of getting control. If he has already hit you, even if it was "just a slap," you are in danger. *Don't fool yourself,* as so many women have done! If he has hit you once, he will inevitably do it again, and the next time it will be harder. Don't accept the excuse that he was drunk or high when he hit you. He hits you because he is a coward or a bully. If he drinks or uses drugs, that's a different problem.

2. YOU HAVE REACHED THE POINT WHERE *YOU* ARE BECOMING PHYSICALLY VIOLENT.
If you have become so frustrated and angry that you have reached a breaking point and have begun to act out your anger in a

physical way, you are also in danger. You could hurt someone seriously, or you could be hurt seriously yourself. Even if your physical acting out does not hurt your abuser physically, you are still being abusive by doing it and you are risking being hurt if he hits you back.

3. YOU HAVE BEGUN TO FANTASIZE ABOUT HARMING OR KILLING YOUR ABUSER.

If you have reached this point, you are feeling trapped and believe there is no way out. But there most certainly is a better way out than risking being put in prison for the rest of your life. He isn't worth it. You need to take responsibility for your anger and find a more constructive way of releasing it. We will discuss ways of doing this in the next chapter and in chapter 9. Making a plan of action so that you can get out of this potentially disastrous relationship will help you feel less trapped and less desperate.

4. YOU ARE SERIOUSLY QUESTIONING YOUR SANITY.

If your abuser is using gaslighting techniques on you or is telling you that you are crazy, your mental health is being jeopardized. The longer you stay in a relationship like this, the more you will doubt yourself, and the stronger the possibility is that you will, indeed, have some kind of emotional breakdown.

5. YOUR CHILDREN ARE BEING ABUSED BY THE ABUSER OR ARE BEING DAMAGED BY YOUR RELATIONSHIP WITH HIM.

Women often fool themselves into thinking that as long as their husbands or boyfriends are not physically or sexually abusing their children, the children are not being damaged. This couldn't be further from the truth. Children are affected by any disruption in the family, and they are severely affected by seeing or hearing their mother be abused in any way. Don't fool yourself into thinking that your children don't know what is going on. They are aware when someone is being cruel or unfair to their mother. They hear you crying, and they know you are unhappy. Not only are your children being damaged in the present by being around abusive behavior, but you are providing them with a poor role model and setting them up to be either victims or victimizers when they grow up.

6. THE ABUSIVE PERSON TOTALLY DEVALUES YOU.

An important element of nearly all emotionally abusive relationships is an inequality of power. This is most often brought about because one person feels superior to the other. When one person is devalued and the other is idealized, the idealized one feels entitled to preferential treatment, which can lead to a controller mentality.

If you are in a relationship with someone who devalues you, looks down on you, and doesn't recognize your worth, then there is little or no hope for the relationship. Ask yourself these questions:

Does this person see me as an equal?

Does he have a general attitude of being superior to me?

Do *I* believe this person is superior to me?

If you answered no to the first question or yes to either or both of the other two, you are in an unequal relationship where you are being devalued by the other person and/or you are devaluing yourself. Any good relationship—whether with your mate, a friend, or a parent—is a relationship of equals. This means that both parties contribute equally to the relationship (even if this is done in entirely different ways), and each person values the other's contribution. For example, while the man in a relationship may make more money, the woman should be equally valued for keeping up the home and taking care of the children. To discover how each of you *honestly* feels about your own and the other's innate value, do the following exercises:

1. Make a list of all the ways you feel that you contribute to the relationship (for example, emotional support, child care, money, social skills, special talents, maintenance of the house or yard, responsibility for the family budget). In a separate room or location, have the other person do the same.
2. After completing this list, make a list of the ways in which you feel the other person contributes to the relationship.
3. Still by yourself, look over both of your own lists and draw whatever conclusions you can. Is one of the lists substantially longer than the other?

4. Now exchange lists and compare how the two of you perceive the situation.

This exercise can be very revealing. It can help you both to see the other person's point of view, *if* you are both open to learning and can approach the experience in a nondefensive way. The other person may be surprised to realize that you contribute so much and so may be able to change his image of you and value you more.

The opposite can also be true, of course. The other person may argue that the things you have written down as your contributions are not all that important or are things that are merely expected in a relationship, or he may otherwise devalue the ways you feel you contribute to the relationship. If this is the case, you may need to seriously consider leaving the relationship.

Taking a Stance

There are only two circumstances that will stop an abuser from continuing to abuse you. The first, and most significant, is when an abuser recognizes that he is abusive and needs to change. However, most emotional abusers are unwilling to look at their problems and have an investment in making their victims feel responsible for any problems in the relationship.

The second way that change can occur is for the victim to refuse to put up with any more abusive behavior. Taking this stance will require you to make a commitment to yourself that you are no longer willing to tolerate abuse, and that you will let your abuser know this. Working on your self-esteem, as described in chapter 9, can help you to strengthen your resolve.

The longer you allow the abuser to get away with mistreating you, the more he will continue to do so. I am *not* inferring that you are in any way responsible for the abuser's behavior. But it has been found that abusers lose more and more respect (if they ever really had any) for the woman who allows the abuse. An emotional abuser will take your silence and compliance as permission to continue to abuse you or to even escalate the abuse, because he knows you will not stop him.

Confronting an Abusive Mate, Parent, or Friend

Although it is understandable that you may be afraid to confront your abuser, it is crucial that you do so, letting him know that you will no longer allow him to abuse you. Since it is more than likely that one of the reasons he is frightening to you is that he reminds you of your original abuser, it is vitally important that you remind yourself that while he may be like your original abuser and treat you in similar ways, he is *not* your original abuser. This is important, because while as a child you were powerless to defend yourself against the abusiveness, as an adult you are not helpless. Even if you *feel* totally trapped and powerless, you are not. You do have the choice to leave.

There are many gentle, caring ways of telling people what you need to tell them while still sounding firm. It is important that you realize that most emotionally abusive people were themselves emotionally abused as children. Although they shouldn't be *blamed* for their actions they should be made aware of their responsibility for those actions. Keep in mind, however, that in some cases it is not safe to confront an abuser.

You have two choices of when to confront the abuser about his behavior: You can wait until the next time he treats you in an offensive way and confront him at that time, or you can set aside time to have a heart-to-heart talk. If you choose to confront your abuser at the next episode of abusive behavior, tell him as directly and sensitively as possible exactly what he has done to offend or hurt you. Abusers are often unaware that they are even being abusive, so it is sometimes best to call them on it right after they have exhibited the offending behavior. The following suggestions will help you to make your confrontation more effective:

☐ Make sure you use "I" messages instead of statements that begin with "you." "I" messages tend to sound less blaming and they make it easier for the other person to hear you nondefensively.

   Example: "I would appreciate it if you wouldn't use that kind of language with me," versus "You have such a foul mouth."

☐ Be specific about how you would like to be treated.

Example: "Would you please confine your criticism of me to the quality of my work, and not about me personally?"
"Would you please not touch me like that?"

If you choose instead to set a time to discuss the situation, plan ahead of time what you are going to say. Also, ask yourself the following two questions before you have the talk:

What do you want to change in the relationship?

What do you know about yourself that might be contributing to the problem?

You could begin the conversation by telling the other person that you read this book, and telling him what you learned about yourself from it.

Example: "You know, when I read this book I realized that I feel abused when you . . . (talk behind my back, criticize me in front of others, seem to continually compete with me)."

You may also want to explain how your personal history influences how you react to the abuser's behavior:

Example: "Part of the reason I feel abused when you do treat me like that is that it reminds me of the way my mother treated me. It pushes my buttons and makes me feel just like I did when I was a kid. I know you probably don't mean to hurt my feelings like this, and I might not even react quite so strongly if I hadn't been treated like that by my mother, but I do feel it is rude and I would appreciate it if you wouldn't continue doing it."

Make sure you don't just blame and complain. In many cases, the other person probably does not intend to hurt you with his behavior. As in the last example, you may want to preface your comments something like this: "I understand that you don't intend to hurt me when you do that, but I want you to know that it does hurt me."

Realize that the abuser may be acting out of habit or because he was treated this way as a child. You could approach this possibility in a sensitive way, such as: "Maybe you could read this book I read about emotional abuse. You were probably mistreated like this yourself as a child, and that's probably where you learned this behavior."

The following suggestions can help you to make your discussion most productive:

☐ Limit yourself to one issue at a time. Don't dump a lot of complaints on the person all at once. This will overwhelm him, cause him to feel extremely defensive, and defeat your purpose.

☐ Avoid labels and name-calling.

☐ Avoid using the words *always* and *never* when describing his behavior.

☐ Take a break if you find yourself getting angry and defensive.

☐ Listen to what the other person has to say before defending yourself. You can gain real understanding of the other person's real feelings and intentions if you give him a chance to explain himself.

☐ Remember that people often have different perceptions of the same reality. You can *both* be right, and no one has to be wrong, if each of you is willing to let the other person have his or her perceptions and if both of you are willing to compromise. I realize that it is very threatening when someone else's reality is extremely different from yours and when that person insists that he is right. But the only real threat is that you could allow someone to take away your reality by letting him make you doubt your own perceptions.

You may want to invest some time and energy in educating the other person, but don't get so caught up in trying to convince him of his problems that you get lost in the relationship again. In addition to explaining how you feel you are being emotionally abused, it may help for you to show him the first part of this book, where I outline what emotional abuse entails.

The outcome of your confrontation can help you to decide whether to continue working on the relationship or to end it. If your abuser is able to hear you without too much defensiveness and is willing to at least consider that his behavior feels abusive to you, then the relationship has a chance. But if he gets immediately defensive, refuses to listen to you, and instead turns the tables and begins attacking you for even bringing up these issues, your relationship may be in serious trouble. On the other hand, you may wish to give it another try later on keeping in mind that he isn't used to you standing up for yourself.

Confronting Your Boss

Obviously, few people feel safe enough to confront an abusive boss about his or her behavior, as tempted as they might be to do so. Unless you are willing to risk your job, you may have to make your confrontation silently to yourself and then work on ways of building up your courage and self-esteem so you can look for another job. You can, however, begin to be more assertive in your present job, as we will discuss in chapter 8.

I suggest you confront your boss only when *all* of the following conditions exist:

☐ Your tolerance limit is exceeded.

☐ If you say nothing, your self-esteem will be greatly damaged.

☐ You can control your emotions.

☐ You can state your complaint or request in a clear, assertive manner.

Rather than saying anything when their tolerance limits are exceeded by an abusive boss, many women take what they think is the easy way out: knuckling under and saying nothing. Often, they are afraid the boss will treat them badly, hold back on raises, or even fire them if he gets angry at them for standing up to him. Thinking that they are powerless to change his mind or his way of managing, they will do or say just about anything to keep him from getting annoyed with them.

Your boss may not be intending to mistreat you, slight you, or fail to deliver on a promise. If you do not bring the issue to his attention, he may never know it exists. Some bosses, on the other hand, try to get away with as much as they can. But once such a boss realizes you are uncomfortable with the way you are being treated, he may respect you more and be willing to rectify the situation. No matter how abusive a boss may be, it is highly unlikely that he will take action against you for speaking up unless you become obnoxious and refuse to back off if he is unwilling to budge.

While under some circumstances keeping your mouth shut is the only prudent course of action, *never* speaking up and always giving in will do you a great deal more harm than good. No job is worth losing your sleep, health, or self-esteem over.

If You Feel You Are a Victim of Sexual Harassment

According to Charles Goldstein, the sexual-harassment expert I mentioned earlier in the book, you should report sexual harassment to a key company executive, perhaps even in writing: "Don't ever just give in, in silence. Get to somebody in the organization who will investigate." If the company is not responsive, then file a complaint with your state's fair employment and housing department or with the federal Equal Employment Opportunity Commission.

In the meantime, you will need to learn ways of asserting yourself so that you do not allow the harassment to continue. In chapter 9, I will discuss ways of becoming more assertive and learning how to say no.

When Is It Best to Leave a Job?

Under any of the following circumstances, it may be best for you to seek other employment:

☐ If you were sexually abused as a child or raped as an adult, and you are now being sexually harassed on the job, you may need to leave the job immediately, regardless of the outcome of the sexual-harassment complaint. It is extremely damaging for victims of sexual abuse to experience sexual harassment of any kind. No matter how much you need the job, it may not be worth it to you to expose yourself to this kind of reabuse. You can still pursue the sexual-harassment case after you have left your job, and you may even decide later to return to your job if your boss is replaced or makes a formal apology to you.

☐ If your boss continues his abusive behavior or even increases it after you have spoken up, it is time for you to leave. If you are not yet in a position to leave, at least begin to make plans to do so.

☐ If your boss is one of the following types of abusers, the chances of his changing his abusive ways is minimal:

Napoleons, bulldozers, destroyers, and controllers. These people feed on power, and the more they get of it, the more they want. Driven to control everything and everyone in sight, they must have the last word and the final authority on any and all decisions, no matter how minor. They are more interested in bossing people around than in getting anything done. If you stand in their way, they will use all their energies to crush you or get rid of you. It doesn't matter to them whether they are right or wrong; what matters is that they are in command.

Antisocial personalities. What Napoleons and controllers attempt to achieve with brute force, the antisocial con artist accomplishes with lies and finesse. As noted earlier, this person will promise you the world and deliver nothing but more promises. Sure, he may throw little "incentives" your way—taking you to lunch or putting on Christmas parties—but he wouldn't dream of paying you what you're worth. Everything this boss does is a form of manipulation to get what he wants. For example, he'll pat you on the back, tell you what a great job you are doing, and then ask you to stay late.

WHAT IF YOU CAN'T DECIDE?

At some point, you *will* need to decide whether you are going to focus your energy on saving the relationship or on preparing yourself for leaving the situation and perhaps ending the relationship completely. If you just can't decide, this may be a good time for you to start therapy. Even though a good therapist will not make your decision for you, she or he can help you to better understand what you really want and need.

Your indecision can be caused by your need to be fair and see the other person's side of the story. Or, if you are codependent, your need to try to change someone else or make him see the light may be keeping you stuck. One of the telltale signs of being codependent is being the only one in a relationship who is working on yourself or admitting your faults. Here is another exercise that can help you in making a decision.

1. List all your reasons for wanting to stay in the relationship.
2. List all your reasons for not wanting to stay.

Good Reasons for Staying:

☐ The abusive person has agreed to go into counseling with me.

☐ He has acknowledged that he has a problem of being emotionally abusive, overcontrolling, and so on.

☐ He recognizes that he is repeating a pattern and is following in his parent's footsteps.

☐ He recognizes that he has an addiction and that it is affecting our relationship. He has joined a self-help group (for example, Alcoholics Anonymous, Sex Addicts Anonymous, Gamblers Anonymous, Debtors Anonymous, or Parents Anonymous).

☐ He has agreed to check himself into a drug or alcohol treatment program, and the whole family is going to receive counseling.

Bad Reasons for Staying:

☐ *"I'm afraid of being alone."*

Betty had been severely emotionally abused by her husband for twenty years. She explained why she had stayed in the relationship so long: "My biggest fear was that of being all alone, of not being able to handle things, of having to take total responsibility for myself. I wasn't sure I could make it by myself."

Some psychologists believe that women's affiliative needs (need to associate with another, typically in a dependent or subordinate position) are stronger than men's. This is because women often have a profound, deep-seated doubt in their own competence, a doubt that began in early childhood. Because of the misguided social expectations and fears of their parents, many girls still believe that they must have protection if they are going to survive.

☐ *"No one else will want me."*

As mentioned in chapter 1, emotional abuse is insidious. It eats away at a woman's self-esteem so gradually that she often doesn't even know the damage she is suffering. After years of hearing an abuser tell her she is ugly, stupid, or incompetent, a woman can be so psychologically destroyed that she believes it. A woman who had been emotionally abused by her boss for ten years said: "My boss always told me, 'You're so stupid—you don't know how to do anything. I don't know why I keep you, except that I'm afraid you couldn't get a job anywhere else, and I know you have a family to support.' After listening to this over and over for years, I really believed him. That belief kept me working far too long for a man who almost drove me crazy."

Because you were deprived of love, nurturing, and security as a child, you may have a "deprivation mentality" in which you always assume that the things you need are in short supply. When someone shows you even the slightest kindness, you react as if the person were giving you a tremendous gift. You are afraid to end a relationship for fear that no one else will ever like you or love you. You believe you should be grateful for what you have because you feel it is all there is.

☐ *"He says he loves me."*

Many emotional abusers are incapable of really loving anyone. They are so caught up in satisfying their own needs that they are unable to even be aware of the other person's needs, much less to satisfy those needs. When we truly love someone, we are able and willing to sometimes put our own needs aside in order to give our loved one what he needs. When we really love someone, we are willing to admit when we are wrong and to work on our problems so that we don't continually keep hurting the other person.

☐ *"I need (him, the job, etc.)."*

Many women are emotionally dependent upon men. As Colette Dowling wrote in her book *The Cinderella Complex,* "There's a kind of panic that many women have about being able to make it in any way other than being dependent on their husbands. They've been taught their whole lives that they can't. It's a conditioning process."

This conditioning is called "learned helplessness." When animals are placed in a situation in which they have no effect on their environment, they begin to give up. New studies show that the same thing happens to humans. If a woman stays long enough in a situation in which she feels she has no control, she loses all hope and stops trying. Only if the woman begins to disengage from her belief in her own helplessness can she break out of the vicious cycle of dependency and its brutal effect on her life.

☐ *"I love him."*

The chances are very high that what you identify as love is dependence, fear of being alone, or need. It is difficult to truly love someone who is constantly hurting you, constantly damaging your self-esteem. When we are being abused, our anger eventually damages and eats away at whatever love we once felt.

The most loving thing you can do is to make the abuser responsible for his behavior. Separation may be the only way to demonstrate that you will no longer put up with the abusive behavior.

☐ *"It really is more my problem than his."*

Typically, an emotionally abused woman attributes the abuser's behavior to some personal inadequacy on her part, or sees it as evidence that she is doing something wrong. She feels responsible for what's going on, and she believes that she must have done something to deserve it. She feels very guilty and ashamed, and she takes on a subordinate role.

☐ *"I am going to work harder on the relationship."*

Instead of reacting to abusive criticism with justified anger, emotionally abused women tend to blame themselves for whatever happens and to look to themselves to improve the situation. They stay in abusive relationships, convincing themselves that if only they cooked better, cleaned the house better, or lost some weight, their husbands would stop being abusive. In a friendship or work situation, the emotionally abused woman convinces herself that if only she was a better friend or employee, the other person would stop his or her abusive behavior.

☐ *"I expect too much from him; from now on I'm going to try to accept him as he is."*

Chances are that you have been doing this for too long already. Emotionally abused women expect themselves to accept the impossible, to be satisfied with next to nothing. You deserve so much more than you are getting already that lowering your expectations will serve only to lower your self-esteem further.

WHAT DO I NEED TO DO BEFORE I'M READY TO LEAVE?

Even though you may know that it is in your best interests to leave the relationship, either temporarily or permanently, you may not feel ready to do so. You may still be suffering from the effects of childhood abuse and thus still lack self-esteem, assertiveness, and a strong sense of self. It is important that you not be critical of yourself for not being able to leave your situation right now. Instead, you need to begin to work on making yourself stronger and on changing your belief system so that you will eventually be able to leave. The following exercise may help you to discover what you need to do to enable yourself to leave:

1. List all the things that are standing in the way of your leaving, including all your fears, doubts, and problems (for example, lack of money, fear of raising your children alone, fear of not being able to get a job, fear of being alone, and so on).

2. Try to determine which of the things you have listed are real considerations, and which are irrational fears. Knowing about your irrational fears is important. As irrational as they may be, it is important that you acknowledge them, otherwise they have a tendency to get out of hand. Facing our irrational fears, bringing them out into the light of day, tends to take away some of their power. As you will begin to discover, most of our irrational fears are manifestations of the deprivation, rejection, and criticism we may have experienced as children.

   Even though Natasha realized that her boss was a carbon copy of her abusive father, and she had completed her unfinished business with her father, she still lacked the self-confidence to go out and look for another job. She needed to build up her self-esteem and gain a stronger sense of self first. She started therapy and began working on these things. After several months of therapy she was far more self-confident and no longer felt so afraid to go on a job interview. Much to her surprise, she got several job offers.

   > I realized that my image of myself had been totally unrealistic. My boss had convinced me that my work was only mediocre, and that I was lucky to have a job at all. But once I got out there, I found that other people valued my work skills and experience. I'm glad I got out of that job when I did. Otherwise, I'd probably have been stuck in it forever, convinced that no one else would ever hire me.

3. Of the things on your list that are real considerations, which of them can you reasonably do something about? Make a list of the ways you could begin to work on each of these items. For example, being able to support yourself is a real consideration. Beginning to set aside grocery money, looking for a job, or going to school to learn a skill are things that many women do to escape from an abusive relationship in which they have become financially dependent upon the abuser.

   Even though you may not be in a position either financially or emotionally to leave at this time, it is important that you decide on a plan of action so that you will be better able to focus your energies. Do this by listing all the things you can begin doing, starting right now, to help you feel able to leave.

Examples:

- ☐ I'm going to start making some new friends.
- ☐ I'm going to enroll in night school.
- ☐ I'm going to start saving money.
- ☐ I'm going to start therapy.

WHAT WILL HE DO IF I DECIDE TO LEAVE?

The abuser will probably try to hang on to you when he senses that you are trying to get away. He is used to having you around to take his frustrations out on and to blame when things go wrong in his life. A typical abuser will try any or all of the following tactics to get you to stay:

- ☐ He will use his best weapons, threats and promises. He may promise he won't ever hurt you again. He may tell you that he has totally changed. But it is important for you to realize that if he were in control of himself in the first place, he would not have been abusive. No matter what he tells you, he can't stop on his own; he needs help. If he tells you he is in control of himself, ask yourself this: If he was in control of his behavior all along, then why did he choose to treat me abusively?

- ☐ He may try to destroy your self-esteem and make you believe you can't survive without him. He may tell you that you are so fat (or dumb, or ugly) that he is the only one who would put up with you. He might try to convince you that you could never get another man. These are all lies, and he does not even believe them himself or he wouldn't feel so threatened.

- ☐ A typical abuser will try to separate his victim from outside support—family, friends, coworkers. If he senses you are going to leave him, he will try even harder to isolate you. You need to break out of your isolation. Join a support group, go back to school, or make new friends so that you can begin to get feedback from people other than the abusive person.

The best reason to leave a relationship is that you have decided that this person or situation is not good for you. And the only time you should stay is if you truly believe that you can now take care of yourself with this person. *There is no virtue in staying in an impossible, destructive relationship or situation.* Making a clean break can be the most courageous act of all.

Whatever decision you make, your focus needs to be on you, not on the abuser. You need to continually work on increasing your assertiveness and your self-esteem and on completing your unfinished business from the past. The next three chapters will help you with these issues.

CHAPTER 7

If You Decide to Stay

"Nobody can make you feel
inferior without your consent."
ELEANOR ROOSEVELT

After confronting the abuser about his behavior, you may have discovered that he is at least somewhat open to accepting the fact that he has a problem. If this is true, there is certainly room for hope.

On the other hand, whether he is willing to admit that he has a problem or not, you may have gained enough strength and determination from confronting him that you have decided you will no longer allow the abuse to continue.

If you have been too afraid to confront, or if you met so much resistance that you backed down, you may have decided to stay only until you can get strong enough to leave.

Choosing to stay in an abusive situation does not mean that you have to continue being abused. No matter what your reason for staying, you will need to continually work on yourself so that you can avoid being abused. Remember that the more abuse you allow, the worse you will feel about yourself. Even if you are staying in the relationship or the job for just a short time, you can't afford any more emotional damage. If you take steps toward becoming more assertive, set your limits and stand by them, release your anger in constructive ways, and continue to work on completing your unfinished business from the past, you have a chance of substantially cutting down the amount of damage that would otherwise come your way.

Many of the issues and techniques we will discuss in this chapter apply to future relationships as well as to your present one. Learning to stand up for yourself will help you to keep future abusers away, because they won't be attracted to someone they can't victimize. In addition, learning and practicing these strategies will help you to keep from inadvertently getting back into an unhealthy pattern of rescuing others or of letting others control or criticize you.

Staying in an Abusive Love Relationship

Each of you has a problem. His is being emotionally abusive, and yours is being willing to accept this abuse. He repeated the cycle of abuse by identifying with the abuser and becoming a victimizer, while you repeated the cycle by identifying with and becoming a victim. Now you must work together in order to make the relationship work, to stop the pattern of abuse, and to make sure you don't pass these roles on to your children.

You have the best chance of making the relationship work if both of you are willing to work on your issues. He needs to recognize that his emotionally abusive behavior has pushed you away from him both physically and emotionally, has caused you to fear him and become defensive, distrustful, and angry, and has damaged your self-esteem. He needs to recognize, too, that it must stop. He also must take total responsibility for his abusiveness and not blame you in *any way*. His abusiveness has been caused by his feelings of inadequacy, low self-esteem, anger, fears, inability to trust, and lack of self, probably brought on by an abusive childhood. You did not in any way *cause* him to be abusive, angry, jealous, possessive, oversexed, or insecure. He came into the relationship with these feelings and tendencies fully developed.

You need to admit that while his emotional abusiveness has indeed damaged you, you also came into the relationship already feeling insecure and inadequate, having difficulty trusting and being intimate.

You may each have exacerbated the other's tendencies to be insecure, abusive, or possessive by pushing buttons and calling forth the past for the other person. You may have added to each other's insecurities, anger, and distrust through rejection, lack of trust, or possessiveness.

Hope Through Therapy

If both people are willing to go into therapy, either as a couple or individually, and both are willing to take responsibility for their part of the problems and for getting the help they need, there may be some hope for the relationship.

The relationship has a better chance of surviving if you are both seeking help in order to work on your individual problems and both have a true desire to grow, rather than seeking help for the sole purpose of saving the relationship. If someone only reluctantly agrees to enter therapy and does not acknowledge internally that he really needs to change, he will tend to be less open to looking at himself honestly and will be more defensive.

Many people are unwilling to go to professional therapists. They may have a negative impression of the profession in general, have had a negative experience in the past, or feel they can't afford it. At the core of all of these reasons is the fear of being exposed or humiliated. If the person who has been abusing you is extremely resistant to therapy, a Twelve-Step program may be less threatening (and is necessary, in any case, if alcohol or drug addiction is involved). There are Twelve-Step programs for alcoholics, drug abusers, sex addicts, compulsive overeaters, adult children of alcoholics, compulsive gamblers, overspenders— nearly every problem that exists.

While entering marital counseling will help you as a couple to learn new ways of relating, more effective communication skills, and better ways of resolving conflicts, what is most important is that you both commit to your own recoveries, whether it is through individual or couple therapy, a support group, or a Twelve-Step program.

If one or both of you have parents who were alcoholics, ACA (Adult Children of Alcoholics) will help you to recover from the emotional abuse you suffered as a result of growing up in an alcoholic family. In ACA you will also learn about the different roles and behaviors children develop as a way of coping with the stress in the family. Some of these roles and behaviors contribute to the difficulties you have in your adult relationships. There are also many excellent books for adult children of alcoholics. Many of these are listed in the recommended reading section at the back of this book.

If you identified with the description of the codependent personality, you may want to attend CODA (Codependents Anonymous) meetings and learn to deal with this tendency. You could also benefit from attending Al-Anon meetings, which are set up for the loved ones and relatives of alcoholics. Even if the person you are involved with is not an alcoholic or drug addict, you will learn ways of dealing with someone who has a problem that causes you distress without constantly nagging at him to change and without trying to rescue him. There are also many books available offering advice on how to recover from codependency, many of which are listed at the back of this book.

WHEN YOU DON'T WANT TO QUIT YOUR JOB

Diane had originally been hired to be the director of finance of a large government agency. After she had been at the agency for a year, there were some major structural changes in the organization, and the division she was heading became two. This essentially meant a demotion for Diane, since both divisions would now be headed up by a new supervisor. While Diane felt good about the lessening of her work load, she was not used to having someone supervise her. The agency was sensitive to this and assured her that the person officially in charge of both divisions would have little or no real control over her, and that it would be business as usual.

But Diane saw trouble from the first day that the new supervisor, Hank, was hired. He began pulling rank on her immediately, asking her to do a menial job that his secretary should have been asked to do. When she stood up for herself and suggested that he assign the task to his secretary, he looked her straight in the eye and said, "I want *you* to do it, and you'll do as I say." From that day on, Diane knew she had a battle on her hands, but it was one that she was willing to fight. She had worked long and hard to recover from the damage caused by her emotionally abusive mother, and she wasn't going to let anyone control her ever again.

Hank continued to load her down with menial tasks. She, in turn, would assign them to a secretary, but even this was time consuming. In addition, Hank began to monitor how often Diane used the telephone for personal calls, how long she took for lunch, and how many sick days she had taken. Because of Diane's position, she had not been required to answer to anyone about these things since she had come to work at the agency. Slowly, Hank was undermining her authority and her self-esteem.

Special financial reports were due at various times of the year, with each report having its own deadline. A big part of Diane's job was to notify Hank of upcoming deadlines. Hank was then responsible for making sure the report was written and for double-checking it before it was mailed. Time after time, Diane would discover that Hank had not even ordered a report to be written, much less double-checked it. A mad scramble would then follow to get the report done, with Diane and other workers often having to work evenings and Saturdays until the report was completed. Needless to say, Diane resented having to work so hard to bail Hank out.

Just before the most important financial report of the year was due, Diane was scheduled for a long-overdue vacation. She was determined not to get stuck bailing Hank out at the last minute this time. Anticipating Hank's procrastination, she notified him of the report long before the deadline and then reminded him weekly. Hank became very resentful, telling her that he knew when it was due and that he wanted her to quit treating him like a child. Diane knew he wouldn't have the report done, but she decided to back off.

At 4:30 in the afternoon on the day before Diane's vacation was to start, Hank called her office in a panic. "Isn't that report due in a couple days?" he asked.

"Yes, Hank, it is," Diane replied calmly.

"Oh my God, it isn't going to be ready. Come into my office right now, and let's get it going!"

Diane took a deep breath and said, "Hank, I'm going home. I'm scheduled for vacation starting tomorrow, and I have a lot of packing to do."

"What do you mean, *vacation?* You can't take a vacation with this report due. Get in here right now!" Hank yelled.

But Diane was not willing to take any more of his emotional abuse. "I'm sorry, Hank, you'll just have to do it yourself this time. I'm leaving for my vacation."

Diane had achieved a major victory. She had communicated to Hank that she wasn't going to continue bailing him out or letting him bully her. While she didn't want to leave her job, because it afforded her opportunities that few other jobs would, she also did not want to be walked all over. She learned to handle Hank in such a way that her self-esteem would not be damaged and her job would not be jeopardized. She continued to be assertive with Hank, and eventually he got the message. He gave up trying to make Diane his flunky and instead began to delegate work to his secretary.

LEARNING TO TAKE CARE OF YOURSELF

Because you have decided to stay in an abusive relationship, like Diane you will need to learn to take care of yourself in much more effective ways than you have up until now. If you are like most emotionally abused women, you probably don't know how to do this very well. You will need to learn the following: how to stop rescuing, how to set your limits and boundaries, how to be assertive, how to release your anger constructively, how to differentiate the past from the present, and how to handle abusive people. While I am going to share with you some basics of assertiveness, effective communication skills, and conflict resolution, I recommend that you expand your knowledge further through therapy, classes, workshops, and further reading.

One of the reasons you have been so attractive to an emotionally abusive person is that it has been clear from the start that you could be manipulated into taking care of him and, furthermore, that you would agree with him that his needs were more important than yours.

Emotionally abusive parents do not usually teach their children how to take care of their own needs. Instead, your parents are much more likely to have taught you how to take care of *their* needs. One of the most important things you can begin to do to take care of yourself is to begin to put your own needs first.

Emotionally abused women do not know how to ask for what they need. They fool themselves into thinking they don't need much, and they don't believe anyone would want to give to them even if they did ask. This is because they received so little as children, and because they were made to feel that it was a tremendous burden for their parents to satisfy their children's needs. When you were a child, you may have received verbal and nonverbal messages from your parents that told you, "I can't meet your needs—I have too many of my own" or "I didn't get *my* needs met when *I* was a child, so you have to take care of me now."

Because of all your prior conditioning, you may believe that taking care of yourself is a very selfish act. But your highest responsibility is to yourself. When you take care of your own needs first, you will be able to be a genuinely caring, giving person, not a martyr thinking everyone owes her or a victim begrudging all that she gives. Although it will be uncomfortable at first, and you may be afraid that others won't like you unless you are giving to them or giving in to them, keep trying. Eventually, you will find that nothing bad happens to you just because you think of yourself first or because you do what *you* want to do.

Stop Rescuing and Enabling

The word *rescue* means "to save, free, release, or recover." To rescue someone also implies that we are saving that person from a present or imminent danger. People generally rescue victims, those who are incapable of being responsible for themselves. But emotionally abused women rescue people who are quite capable of taking care of themselves. They rescue people from their responsibilities by taking care of their responsibilities for them.

The word *enable* means "to provide the means or opportunity, empower, permit, allow, or facilitate." The term *enabler* was originally used to describe the husband or wife of an alcoholic who allowed, or even encouraged, the alcoholic to continue drinking. Any act that helps an alcoholic continue drinking, prevents him from suffering consequences, or in any way makes it easier for him to continue drinking is considered an enabling behavior. We will use the term *enabler* to refer to someone who encourages or makes it possible for an emotionally abusive person to continue an abusive behavior, and we will use the term *enabling* to refer to any destructive form of helping. (It is interesting to note that the opposite of enable is "to forbid, prohibit, hinder, or prevent." In essence, if you stop allowing the abuser to continue his harmful behavior, you are in actuality preventing or forbidding it.)

One of the many problems with rescuing or enabling is that we set ourselves up to eventually be the victim. As we become more tired and needy ourselves, we inevitably become resentful of and angry at the person we are rescuing. Since he doesn't need our help in the first place and probably didn't ask for it, he's not only not going to be appreciative of it but will probably experience it as meddlesome. We begin to notice that he hasn't taken our advice, and is not changing, as we had expected. We feel used, hurt, and unappreciated.

Rescuing or enabling is *not* an act of love. We don't rescue because we love; we rescue because we want to gain a false sense of control over someone else. We rescue because we are repeating a pattern from childhood as a way of avoiding our feelings of helplessness. We rescue because we assume the other person can't handle the responsibility of his own feelings, because we can't tell the truth, because we can't say no, or because we are afraid the other person will get angry with us. And, most important, we rescue because we don't feel good about ourselves. We don't feel lovable, so we settle for being needed. We don't feel good about ourselves, so we feel compelled to be "good" by rescuing someone else.

If your abuser is an alcoholic, drug addict, sex addict, or compulsive gambler or spender, you may assume that he can't get over his problems without your help. In reality, he will probably do much better without your help, and without someone else to depend on and blame for his problems.

The best thing you can do for yourself and for him is to back off and let him take care of himself. Leave him alone to face his feelings and suffer the consequences of his actions. Don't take these opportunities for growth away from him. Allow him to be responsible and accountable for himself *and* take care of your needs and wants sometimes.

Establish Limits and Boundaries

Part of learning to trust yourself to take care of yourself is to build and maintain healthy boundaries. We all need to have a private psychological space that belongs to us and to us alone. This space is both physical and emotional. On the physical level, each of us has a "comfort zone," a given space between ourselves and others that enables us to feel comfortable and unthreatened. For example, if someone invades your "space" by standing too close to you, you feel threatened and need to move away from that person.

Your comfort zone will differ depending on who you are dealing with. When it is a stranger, you will probably need a great deal more space than you do when your lover is near. One client of mine noticed,

> I need more space between myself and my father than I need with my close friends. This is because I still have a fear of him becoming sexual with me, as he did in the past. I am not afraid of my friends "invading my space," so I allow them to be physically closer to me.

Most of us start a relationship thinking we have certain limits in terms of what we will or won't tolerate from other people. But as the relationship progresses, we tend to move our boundaries back, giving in more and more until we end up tolerating more and more and even doing things we were determined not to do.

Not only do we begin tolerating unacceptable and abusive behavior, we begin to convince ourselves that these behaviors are normal or acceptable. We begin to believe the abuser when he tells us that we deserve this behavior because of how we act.

We have to set limits on what we will allow others to do to us. The people we relate to need to know we have boundaries. If you continue giving your power and control over to the abuser, you can be sure that he will abuse it. Not only do we need to set boundaries and limits in terms of what we allow others to do *to* us, we need to set limits on what we will allow ourselves to do *for* other people. Doing the following sentence-completion exercise will help you to set your limits and establish your boundaries. Write your answers down on paper, taking as much time as you need.

☐ What behavior are you no longer willing to tolerate?

Complete the following sentences:

1. I will no longer allow_____.
Examples:

   ☐ I will not allow anyone to physically or sexually abuse me.

   ☐ I will not allow anyone to emotionally abuse me by verbally assaulting me, making me doubt my perceptions, etc.

2. I won't have a relationship with someone who _____.
Examples:

   ☐ I won't have a relationship with someone who is unfaithful to me.

   ☐ I will not have a relationship with someone who refuses to get help for his problems.

You can get clues to what boundaries you need to set by paying attention to the things you complain about the most, the things you are sick of, and the things you make threats about. For example, if you keep threatening to leave the relationship if your husband has one more affair, then that is a boundary you need to set. If you have had it with your friend gossiping about you, that is a limit you need to set.

Here are some examples of limits set by some of my clients:

I will not have sex with someone who is sleeping around.

I will not allow criminal behavior in my house.

I will not allow drugs in my home.

I will not rescue people from the consequences of alcohol or drug abuse.

I will not enable my husband by paying off his gambling debts.

I will not rescue anyone in my household from the consequences of his or her irresponsible behavior.

I will not lie to protect someone else.

Stick to your boundaries, and enforce them. The important thing is that you mean what you say and say what you mean. Be consistent, and don't back down. Don't let others manipulate you into feeling guilty so that you remove your boundary and let them abuse you once again.

In an attempt to change her tendency to be a codependent, Loretta made it clear to her brother, a compulsive gambler, that if he got into trouble financially because of his gambling she would not lend him any more money. Sure enough, several months later, he called her up begging to borrow some money to make his house payment. Even though it was very difficult for her, Loretta stuck to her resolve not to help him. In spite of his pleading, in spite of the fact that she knew he might lose his house, she refused to bail him out. She felt good about being able to enforce this boundary, even though her brother was furious with her. She had come to realize that she was only enabling his gambling by bailing him out time after time.

The emotional abuser will test you to see whether you are serious or will change your mind. After all, since you haven't meant what you have said in the past and have made so many empty threats, it is natural that he won't believe you right away. But over time, it will become more and more clear that you do mean what you say.

You do not need to be inflexible. Your boundaries can change as you grow and change and can trust yourself more to honor the limits you have set.

Learn and Practice Assertiveness

Determining how you can communicate your limits and needs to the abusive person can seem like an insurmountable problem. It will require assertiveness, a skill that many women lack. From childhood you have probably been developing attitudes that inhibit assertiveness. You may have many of these beliefs and fears:

If I ask for what I want, people will think I am selfish.

It's better to be liked than to speak up and be seen as a troublemaker.

It's better to just put up with things than to rock the boat.

Women who assert themselves are being pushy and aggressive.

What other people think is more important than what I think.

You can assert yourself and still respect the feelings and rights of other people. You can express your feelings without being obnoxious. Being assertive is not being aggressive, pushy, or selfish. It is being able to state your views and desires directly, honestly, and spontaneously, to act without indecision, and to be true to yourself.

Here is a common work situation: Your boss comes to you five minutes before lunch and asks you if you will do a rush job for her. She does this kind of thing often, and while you have usually done as she requests (resentfully, I might add), this time you have a lunch date.

One nonassertive thing to do would be to cancel your lunch date and enable your boss to continue her inconsiderate, crisis-oriented behavior. Another way of handling the situation non-assertively would be to apologize profusely for having a lunch date, acting as though you're doing something wrong by not dropping what you're doing to bail her out. The *assertive* thing to do would be to handle it somewhat like this: you say, "I already have a lunch appointment, so I won't be able to help you out this time. I realize you're rushed, and I'll be happy to do the work as soon as I get back."

Many people get confused about the purpose of speaking up. They feel that unless the other person hears their point of view and accepts it, it was a wasted effort. However, the purpose of speaking up is not to change the other person's point of view, but merely to assert yours. In some sense, it doesn't matter whether the other person even heard you, much less was persuaded by you. What matters is that you were able to speak your mind, that you didn't squelch your ideas and feelings. Once you begin to assert yourself without any expectations, you will gain more self-esteem and the courage to continue speaking up.

If you haven't already taken an assertiveness-training class, by all means do so (and if you have already taken one consider doing it again as a refresher course). Assertiveness training will help you to learn your rights as a human being and will give you practice in standing up for yourself. It can give you courage you never knew you had, and it can teach you how to speak your mind without being defensive or offensive. Inquire at a college or university, the local chapter of the National Organization for Women (NOW), or a mental-health association.

Assertiveness training teaches people to express both positive and negative feelings openly and directly. It is most helpful for the following people: those who cannot express anger or irritation, those who have difficulty in saying no, those who are overly polite and allow others to take advantage of them, those who find it difficult to express affection and other positive responses, and those who don't feel they have a right to express thoughts, beliefs, and feelings. The goals of assertiveness training are to increase your repertoire of behaviors in order to give you more choices and to teach you to express yourself in a way that reflects sensitivity for the feelings and rights of others.

While assertiveness training is helpful for many emotionally abused women, it isn't for everyone. Some women need to learn to like themselves enough to *want* to stand up for themselves. For these women, the ability to be assertive comes after they have spent time in therapy or recovery, continually working on their unfinished business, and spent a great deal of time parenting and nurturing themselves.

Erin, a woman who had been severely emotionally, physically, and sexually abused as a child, told me why she didn't want to learn how to be assertive: "I don't like conflict. I'd rather do whatever I have to do to keep the peace than to risk an argument. It just isn't worth it to me." Anyone with a background like Erin's would naturally be reluctant to speak up for herself. Erin needed to focus on healing from her wounds and building up her inner strength so that she could feel strong enough to risk conflict.

JUST SAY NO!   Another aspect of assertiveness is learning to say no. This is basic to getting rid of a victim mentality, and it will help set the stage for you to be able to stand up to even the most abusive of people. Start by saying no quietly to yourself when you are alone in your house or car. Imagine that you are saying no to the abuser. Say it softly at first, and gradually build up to a scream. This will strengthen your resolve to not allow yourself to be abused again and will give you the courage to stand up for yourself.

Start saying no to people who want something from you, beginning with those who are the least threatening. Practice with telephone solicitors or door-to-door salesmen, and work your way up to saying no to a friend who wants a favor you'd rather not do. Find out how good it feels to take care of your own needs first and to gain the kind of self-respect that comes from no longer being a doormat. The good feelings you get from doing this may give you the encouragement you need to tackle more difficult situations. Over time, you will gain the ability to say no to your current abuser.

Clara practiced saying no even when she didn't necessarily feel very strongly about the situation. For instance, if a friend called to ask if she wanted to go somewhere and Clara did not feel strongly about it either way, she would say no. In the past, she had always said yes whenever she didn't care much either way. She had been so used to doing what others wanted that she really didn't know her own desires. Saying no actually helped her to learn what she really wanted to do. Sometimes, after she had said no automatically, she found that she really *did* want to go, after all. Just giving herself permission to say no opened the door for her to find out what she really wanted.

Finally, Clara was ready to tackle the big challenges of saying no to needy friends and to the people she cared about the most, her boyfriend and her mother. For Clara, saying no to friends who seemed to be in need was difficult, because she remembered how many times she had needed someone when she was a child and no one had helped. But she gradually realized that she couldn't change her past by rescuing others. And the more she learned to take care of her own needs, the less she needed to rescue others. She also learned that others can, and do, take care of themselves when they need to, and that by rescuing her friends so often she was actually enabling them to continue being victims themselves.

Learning to say no to her boyfriend and mother was more difficult. Clara discovered that she was afraid to say no to them out of fear of rejection. She believed that the only way anyone would love her was if she did what that person wanted. Clara had learned to be compliant from her mother, who had allowed Clara's abusive stepfather to walk all over her. If she and her mother did everything he wanted, then he "loved" them. If they didn't, he ignored them. Learning to say no to those she loved was the ultimate challenge for Clara. But she decided she had to take the risk—she had to find out if they would love her even if she didn't always do what they wanted her to do.

Fortunately, she discovered that they *did* love her in spite of her newfound ability to say no and take care of herself first. At first her mother tried to manipulate her into giving in, but she soon discovered that when Clara said no, she meant it. Her mother pouted and stayed away for a while, but when she came back she had a different attitude toward Clara. Clara described the change: "She still asks me for things, but not as often. And when she does, she says, 'Of course, I understand if you don't want to.'"

Surprisingly, Clara's boyfriend was actually pleased with the changes in her. It turned out that he had always been uneasy about her willingness to just "go along" with whatever he wanted to do. He explained,

> I was never sure whether she really wanted to do something or was just trying to please me. This made me feel like she would do anything I wanted, and that made me disrespect her. I like her much better now, and I find I trust her more, too. Now, when she says she wants to do something, I believe her—I know she really wants to do it.

It is crucial that you learn to say no instead of making up excuses, justifications, and rationalizations. You don't have to explain yourself all the time. It is enough that you do not want to do something simply because you don't want to do it. If you feel like it, you can accompany your refusal with a simple, straightforward explanation of what you are feeling. Anything more than that leaves you open to further challenge. By all means, do not say "I'm sorry, but . . . " when you say no. This can weaken your stand, and the other person may be tempted to play on your guilt. When you have decided that the best thing to do is to say no, you have nothing to be sorry about.

When practicing saying no, keep these points in mind:

☐ Not being able to say no can leave you exhausted. Instead of thinking of excuses for why you can't do something, just say no. It really works.

☐ Remember, your intention in saying no is not to hurt the other person but to help yourself.

☐ Know that at first it will be uncomfortable to say no, but with some practice it will begin to feel great.

Release Your Anger in Constructive Ways

Anger has probably played a key role in the abusive relationship you are now in. A great deal of the abuse you have suffered has been a result of the abuser's anger. Although the person who is being abusive to you may, indeed, be angry with you at times, more than likely he is just using you as a depository for all his built-up rage and anger—because he was abused as a child, because his job isn't working out, because he hates himself for his addiction to alcohol, drugs, sex, or gambling, or because he feels bad about himself for other reasons.

Because you have been continually emotionally abused, you, too, have become very angry. Whether you have expressed this anger or not, it is there nonetheless. Even if you aren't shouting, even if you are trying to pretend you aren't angry, you *are* angry. And even if you aren't aware that you are angry, rest assured that others around you know it. You give yourself away with your dirty looks, sighs, sarcasm, or angry silences.

Sometimes you may "lose it" and blow up. You can't take it any more, so you go on a tirade—yelling, name calling, threatening to leave. But nothing gets accomplished. The abuser knows it will all blow over, and he knows you won't really leave. You lost your credibility a long time ago. You are left with your guilt over losing control, causing such a fuss, and stooping to his level, and he is left with a feeling of superiority because you became so "hysterical."

Or, perhaps you have started to get angry, only to have your anger squelched by the abuser. His attitude is this: "How *dare* you get angry with *me*? I'm the boss around here. I'll get angry with you if I want, but don't you dare get angry with me." This may have caused you to slink back to your corner, thinking to yourself that he was right—who did you think you were to get angry, anyway?

Because anger is such a powerful emotion, it is difficult for many women to express it. Many women are afraid that anger will lead to violence, and in fact they have often seen this happen. You may have witnessed your mother being beaten because she dared stand up to your father. Or someone may have hit or abused you when angry. In addition, you may have experienced yourself close to losing control. But there are many forms of anger, and hostility and violence are only two of them.

Anger is a legitimate feeling that may be expressed in passive, indirect, aggressive, or assertive ways.

We are being passive with our anger when we express annoyance or irritation without really admitting that we are feeling angry. In fact, if someone were to ask us if we are angry we would probably deny it and say, "Oh, no, I'm just frustrated" or "No, but he sure can annoy me."

Another form of anger is indirect anger. This is when we deny that we are angry but try to make the other person feel guilty. We can also express our anger in other indirect ways, such as withholding affection or sex. Sometimes the only way a woman who feels powerless can communicate her resentment is by "holding out" sexually. (Also, as I mentioned in the first part of the book, it is often impossible to feel sexual toward someone who is emotionally abusing you because you feel angry and because you don't feel safe or comfortable in being that vulnerable.)

And then there is aggressive anger or rage. Rage seldom has anything to do with the problem at hand. It is anger that has built up over time, that gets stirred up by having our buttons pushed. Rage is intensified, exaggerated anger that can be very frightening and can become violent.

There is, of course, a happy medium between homicidal rage and passivity. This happy medium is assertive anger. Assertive anger, unlike passive or indirect anger, is expressed clearly and directly. And unlike aggressive anger, it is not verbally or physically abusive.

People sometimes mistakenly think they are being assertive by complaining. Even though you may think that you have been releasing your anger toward your abuser, you probably haven't been doing it in a very constructive or effective way. Nagging at someone is not the same as ventilating your anger. In fact, constant nagging or complaining can prolong your anger. The more you nag, the more helpless and ineffectual you feel and the more anger you build up.

Here are some steps to take to help you deal with your anger in an assertive, constructive way:

1. *Recognize your anger.* Women tend to deny their anger because they don't believe they have a valid reason for it, and because they have been conditioned to believe that it is "unladylike" to get angry. They feel that anger is always aggressive or unreasonable.

2. *Feel the emotion of anger in your body.* Anger is energy, and as such it can be a motivating force to empower those who feel helpless.

3. *Feel any underlying emotions of hurt or fear.* Emotions come in layers. Sometimes anger is covered up by fear and hurt; at other times, the opposite is true. When we allow ourselves to feel one emotion, it makes it possible for us to access our other emotions as well.

4. *Acknowledge the thoughts that accompany your feelings.* If at all possible, say these thoughts out loud. Don't judge your thoughts,

no matter how embarrassing or crazy they may seem. Realize that you don't have to act on your thoughts just because you have them, and that by allowing yourself to vent them you are making it possible to let go of them much more easily.

5. *Identify the source of your anger.* This may actually be harder than you think. While you may assume that you are angry at your current abuser, you may actually be angry at your original abuser. Watch for patterns and repetitive situations.

   In addition, be aware that rescuing breeds anger. If we haven't set proper limits and boundaries and learned to say no, we may build up so much anger and resentment that we become angry at anyone who needs or requests anything from us. If someone is in need, we feel we have to help, but we feel resentful while doing it.

6. *Take a look at why you are angry.* It may feel more convenient to get angry over something small rather than facing the real cause of your anger. For example, while you may tell yourself you are angry at your friend for calling and waking you up in the morning, in actuality you are angry with her because when she calls she only talks about herself and never asks you how you are. Your real anger at her has been building up for some time, but since you haven't expressed it, it is coming out over something far less important.

7. *Decide what action, if any, you need to take.* You may need to tell the person you are angry with what he has done to anger you. A lot of our anger is triggered by unmet needs. You need to figure out what you need from that person and ask him for it. If he can't, or won't, give it to you, then you must figure out what you need to do next to take care of yourself.

8. *Take responsibility for constructively releasing your anger.* If you cannot talk to the person you are angry with (because he is not available or won't listen, or because you are too angry to talk), you may need to find another way to express your anger. Write the person a letter that you do not intend to mail. Get all your thoughts and feelings down on paper without censoring them. Put your head in a pillow and scream. Pound the bed with your fists. Physically releasing your anger is very beneficial, especially when you can't find the right words to express your feelings.

Obviously, it is not going to be possible for you to release your anger directly at work. But there are other ways to constructively ventilate your anger toward a boss or coworker. Here are a few suggestions:

☐ On your lunch hour or at home, have an imaginary conversation with your abusive boss or coworker. If you can find some privacy (some of my clients have gone to their cars and rolled up the windows), talk out loud. Tell the person everything you would like to say, holding nothing back.

☐ Write a letter that you do not mail, telling the person exactly how you feel. (For obvious reasons, it is best to write this letter at home.) Read the letter out loud as if you were reading it to your boss or coworker, then tear it up.

☐ Take a walk on your lunch hour and imagine that you are stomping on your abusive boss or coworker with every step you take.

Since you have lived with your unexpressed anger for years, you may have to go through an "angry phase" in which you get angry a great deal of the time. This phase, which usually lasts only a few months, will pass once you have released a lot of your pent-up anger and learned to deal with your anger in more constructive ways.

If you continue to have difficulty expressing your anger, react violently to minor annoyances, have thoughts about hurting yourself or others, or often become severely depressed, I recommend that you seek help from a professional therapist.

BE WILLING TO LET THE OTHER PERSON GET ANGRY, TOO. When you establish your boundaries and begin to stand up for yourself, it is inevitable that the other person may get angry with you. After all, he is probably not used to your being so assertive. Just as you need to accept your own anger, you will need to accept his righteous anger as well, with emphasis on the word *righteous.* Emotional abusers are often irrationally and unfairly angry so much of the time that it can be difficult to accept any of their anger. However, as long as they don't respond by being verbally or physically abusive, it is important to let them have their say.

Learn to Differentiate the Past from the Present

Your current abuser may be constantly pushing your buttons and reminding you of the past and of your original abuser. But as much as he may be like your original abuser, he is not that person. Work on making that distinction. You cannot hold your current abuser responsible for what your original abuser did. In addition, it will help you to feel less intimidated by your current abuser if you aren't mixing him up with your original abuser. If you can make this distinction, you will be less frightened of your current abuser's anger and will respond to it like an adult instead of a cowering child. The following suggestions can help you:

☐ Make a list of all the ways in which your current abuser is different from your original abuser.

☐ Whenever you are intensely engaged with your current abuser, whether it is in an argument or during lovemaking, make sure that you look at his face and remind yourself that he is *not* your original abuser. Whenever a situation triggers memories of previous abuse, we can become confused temporarily and feel we are dealing with an original abuser. If a woman was sexually abused as a child she may have flashbacks to the abuse during lovemaking. Focusing on her lover's face can often bring her back to reality and to the present.

A few weeks after starting her new job, Cassandra began to have symptoms she hadn't had for years. She had difficulty sleeping, she became very withdrawn from her friends, and her appetite disappeared. When she came in to see me for her weekly visit, she told me, "I don't know what's wrong with me. I thought I was just about ready to stop therapy, but now it seems as though nothing has changed at all. I feel just like I used to feel when I was a kid."

During the session we were able to figure out that what was upsetting her was her new boss. He reminded her of her step-father, who had been extremely cruel to her. Once Cassandra understood why she had become so upset, she was able to reassure herself that she had no rational reason to be petrified of her boss, that it was her stepfather she was afraid of, and that, in fact, it was her inner child who was afraid, not her adult self. Since she had already released a great deal of her anger toward her stepfather and had even confronted him in a fantasy confrontation, she was not as afraid of him anymore. The more Cassandra reminded herself that her boss was not her stepfather and that she was not trapped in the job like she had been in her home as a child, she recognized more and more of the differences between her boss and her stepfather and grew much more comfortable with her boss.

Each of us has buttons that get pushed, things that are said that remind us of things our original abuser may have said to us. These buttons can send us into a tizzy without warning. Sometimes others know what buttons to push to hurt our feelings because we have shared our past with them and told them the things that bother us. At other times, someone may say something that causes us pain without realizing that he is upsetting us. I have listed some of the "buttons" that tend to most upset those who were emotionally abused as children:

☐ Being told you are a liar

☐ Being told you are crazy

☐ Being told you don't know what you are talking about

☐ Being told you are stupid

☐ Being told you are unreliable or untrustworthy

☐ Being told you are fat, skinny, ugly, and so on

Make a list of your own "buttons." The next time someone uses one of these phrases, tell him that you do not want him to use it again, that it hurts you deeply and reminds you of the abuse you sustained as a child. If the other person seems to be sympathetic, you may wish to share your entire list, explaining why each phrase upsets you so much. While you are at it, you might want to ask the other person to make up a button list and share it with you.

Obviously, it requires a great deal of trust on your part to share this kind of information, since knowing your particular buttons can give another person ammunition with which to deliberately hurt you. If you have not established this kind of trust, by all means do not set yourself up for any more hurt by sharing this information.

Our buttons can be pushed at any time and by anyone. Tess had worked as a keypunch operator for the same company for eleven years. Her company was installing a new machine, and Tess was terrified that she would not be able to learn the new system and would get fired.

The company hired someone who knew the new system to be in charge of the training. Just out of college, the new employee felt superior to the older women she was to train, many of whom did not have any college education. She had no patience for those she felt weren't catching on fast enough. Sometimes she even explained things too quickly and left out important information. When she was asked to clarify something, she answered the question in such a way as to imply that anyone with half a brain would have understood it in the first place. The women she was training were angry with her. Some of them even thought she was deliberately making it hard for them, perhaps because she was afraid that if they got too good she would lose her authority.

Instead of recognizing that the trainer was the one with the problem and becoming angry like the rest of the employees, Tess became paralyzed with fear whenever she didn't understand something. This was because when she was a child, her mother had frequently accused her of being stupid. She would tell her to do a chore around the house but would neglect to teach her how to do it. When Tess would ask her a question about how to do something, her mother would yell at her for being so stupid. Then, if Tess didn't do the chore correctly, her mother would slap her and tell her again how stupid she was.

Tess began to break down and cry every time she didn't understand something during the training, and she would fret for hours after each training session. Tess's buttons had been pushed, not so much by words, but by the superior attitude and domineering behavior of her trainer.

Tess's behavior became so irrational that her supervisor finally suggested that she get some counseling from the company therapist. During one of her counseling sessions she was able to make the connection between the present situation and her past. With this valuable information, Tess was able to remind herself that her trainer was not her mother. Further counseling, coupled with some assertiveness-training classes, gave Tess the courage to begin asking her trainer to clarify information whenever she became confused.

LEARNING HOW TO HANDLE ABUSIVE PEOPLE

The abusive person in your life may not change much, so you will have to. The following strategies may help you to deal more effectively with even the most abusive of people.

Disarming an Angry Person

When an abuser is screaming at you, try the following exercise to disarm his anger:

1. Acknowledge that you hear him by saying, "I know you are angry at me." This kind of acknowledgment will often calm the person enough to enable you both to discuss the issue.
2. If this doesn't work, in a calm, assertive manner say something like, "I really want to talk to you, but I can't talk to you when you're yelling. As soon as you're calm, I'll be happy to talk to you." Repeat this until the person calms down. Then listen to what he or she has to say.
3. If the screaming continues, you have a right to leave the situation. You might want to tell the person that you are leaving for a while, and that you will return when things have cooled off.

Dealing with Criticism: Verbal Self-Defense

Learning how to defend yourself against verbal assaults will help you to stop being victimized and will be a big boost to your self-esteem. Instead of taking in whatever criticism is dished out to you, you can begin to see it for what it is—an expression of the other person's insecurity, jealousy, or need to control. Instead of having your confidence worn away by constant criticism, you can deflect the attacks back to the person who is doing the criticizing. Following are some pointers for handling criticism:

KNOW WHEN YOU ARE BEING CRITICIZED.   Pay attention to how you feel when you are talking to someone who has a history of being critical of you. Notice when your stomach gets tight or when you feel a sinking sensation in your stomach. Notice any mood changes on your part. For example, if you have been feeling happy and light and suddenly become depressed, try to remember what has just been said to you. You may have been a victim of a put-down without even realizing it. The same can be true if you have been feeling confident and spontaneous but suddenly feel insecure and are now guarding your words.

MAKE THE ASSUMPTION THAT MOST INSULTING REMARKS, EVEN WHEN COUCHED AS "CONSTRUCTIVE CRITICISM," MEAN LESS ABOUT YOU THAN ABOUT THE PERSON DOING THE CRITICIZING.   The person may be projecting his own low self-image onto you, taking out his frustrations on you, or needing to put you down for some reason (probably because he is angry with you or envious of you). Don't assume that what he is saying has any relevance to you at all. You are already hard enough on yourself. You don't need someone else telling you what is wrong with you and damaging your already low self-esteem. If the person has something he wants to tell you and his intentions are to work out problems in the relationship, he can do so without insulting you.

TRY NEVER TO GET INTO A VERBAL BATTLE WITH AN EMOTIONAL ABUSER.   He will inevitably win the argument because he's so good at zeroing in on your insecurities. Most emotional abusers are like defense attorneys: no matter what you say, they will somehow turn it back on you. Exchanging insults can easily get out of hand, sometimes even escalating into physical violence.

TRY OUT A VARIETY OF STRATEGIES UNTIL YOU FIND JUST THE RIGHT ONE TO SUIT THE OCCASION.   For instance:

- [ ] Be as direct as you can and give the remark back to the person criticizing you.

   Examples:
   "Are you aware that that remark hurt my feelings?"
   "I'm sure you didn't mean to insult me."

- [ ] Ask the person to clarify the remark.

   Examples:
   "Did I understand you correctly when you said _____?"
   "What did you mean by that?"

- [ ] Let the person know you have noticed the remark but have decided not to respond to it directly. For example, say "Oh!" as if something has surprised you. Or say "Ouch," registering your hurt but saying nothing else. Criticizers are much more careful when they know you know.

- [ ] Extinguish the criticism by yawning or looking away. Criticizers are trying to get your attention, so they hate it if they think that what they are saying is boring to you.

- [ ] Use your humor to agree with everything the person has said.

   Example:
   Criticizer: "This room is a mess. Aren't you ever going to get organized?"
   You: "Probably not. If I haven't gotten organized by now, I guess I'm not going to!"

- [ ] Confront the criticism head on. Tell the criticizer face-to-face or in a letter that you are not going to absorb any more of his criticism. When he criticizes you, you could ask him why he wants to hurt you, yawn or close your eyes, or just walk away.

In her book *You Know I Wouldn't Say This If I Didn't Love You,* Jennifer James, Ph.D., suggests that you tell the criticizer that you'll allow only one criticism per telephone call, and that you'll hang up after he gives you two. If it is someone you love, she suggests that you say, "I love you" just before you hang up. She also suggests you do the same with correspondents, notifying the criticizer that you will allow only one criticism per letter, and that after one criticism you'll cut off the rest of the letter and mail it back.

Most people do not know just how critical they are. They may be repeating the pattern of being critical that their parents modeled, and they may even be repeating the very same criticisms that they were given when they were children without being aware of it. When you confront someone about the fact that he is being critical, he will probably become quite defensive. He may say something like "I am just being honest" or "I'm just trying to help you." If you get this kind of defense, tell the person that he doesn't need to take on the responsibility for your life, that you are an adult who is fully capable of taking care of yourself, and that you can get all the information about yourself that you need in a less painful way.

Try to listen objectively to what you and the other person are actually saying to each other. You may want to tape-record some of your conversations and arguments in order to hear what you both sound like. You may be surprised to hear your words and your tone of voice. This is also a good way to let the other person hear himself, although you should do it only with his permission.

By practicing the techniques in this chapter you will be able to discover strengths you never knew you had. This will enable you to take care of yourself better in your current relationships and to defend yourself against abuse, as well as to develop the strength and courage to leave a relationship that is damaging to you.

P A R T

4

A TIME TO HEAL

Taking Time for Yourself

"Nothing can bring you peace
but yourself."

RALPH WALDO EMERSON,
Self-Reliance

All of us travel through life with only one constant companion, and that is ourself. How sad if your closest companion is someone you don't even know.

Whether you leave your current relationship or stay in it, it is vital that you discover who you are, separate from *any* relationship. You've been hiding from yourself by getting lost in one abusive relationship after another, and now you need to take some time to put your life in perspective, to heal from your past relationships, and to do some deep inner reflection. As scary as the prospect may seem, you need time alone to discover who you really are, to learn to rely on yourself, to learn to like your own company, and to break your tendency to be dependent on others.

Taking the time to be alone will help you to gather the courage to leave an abusive relationship, to avoid abusive relationships in the future, and to discover what you want and need out of life. From this position you will be less needy, less desperate to immediately attach yourself to someone in an attempt to avoid yourself.

If you have already ended your most recent abusive love relationship, it is crucial that you do not get involved in another romantic relationship for at least six months. This may sound like an awfully long time, but I can guarantee you that if you don't spend at least this much time alone—working on your own issues in therapy, attending assertiveness-training classes, building up your self-esteem, and, most important, getting to know yourself—you will find yourself in yet another abusive relationship, repeating the same pattern.

We cannot be intimate with another person until we are able to be intimate with ourselves. In order to be intimate with another person we must first establish our own identity and know who we are and what we feel, prefer, and want. If we do not know these things about ourselves, we cannot share them with another person. If we are unaware of ourselves, there is no way we can express ourselves to someone else.

The more time you spend away from your abusive relationship, the more objective you will be and the better able to recognize just how abusive it was. As my client Felicia told me, "The longer I am away from Jake, the more I realize how abusive he was. While I was in the relationship I would get so caught up in our conflicts that I couldn't see the relationship realistically."

You will also get a chance to observe relationships that are not abusive and to see that there is another way to live. Felicia continued: "As I am around people who treat me better and am exposed to couples who treat each other with respect and consideration, I can see just how abusive my relationship was. I put up with Jake's abuse because I thought it was normal."

The time you take to be alone now may be the only time you have ever stood alone, not depending on anyone else to help hold you up. Your fear of being alone has propelled you into continually seeking relationships and staying in destructive ones. You need to know that you can be alone and be happy with yourself. That way, you will never stay in an abusive relationship again out of fear of being alone.

LOOKING FOR LOVE IN ALL THE WRONG PLACES

Because of your low self-esteem, you, like many emotionally abused women, have been searching for something outside yourself to give you a sense of completion and a sense of being worthwhile. And, like many women in our culture, you have probably looked to love to make you feel worthy and whole, seeing romance as the solution for your feelings of incompleteness and inadequacy. From an early age, most females in our society have been taught that, as the song goes, "you're nobody till somebody loves you."

We search endlessly for that one true love, that person we can merge with, that person who will complete us—that one special person who will take away our feelings of self-dislike, desperation, and estrangement. But no two people can merge, no matter how great the urge to do so. Sheila Graham, who had a destructive affair with F. Scott Fitzgerald, wrote about her relationship with him and in so doing revealed how she sought completion through the fantasy of merging with another:

> I looked into his face, searching it, trying to find its mystery, its wonder for me, and I said, almost prayerfully, "If only I could walk into your eyes and close the lids behind me, and leave all the world outside."

Heterosexual women are not the only ones who search for completion through romantic love. Lesbian women, too, feel compelled to be in one romantic relationship after another because they feel incomplete and worthless without one. Although they may not be hooked on male approval, they can be just as addicted to the approval and love of a "significant other."

But the truth of the matter is that you are nobody until *you* love you. In the next chapter I will discuss ways of raising your self-esteem. But before you can raise your self-esteem, you must first discover who you are, and the only way to do this is to spend time with yourself.

As young girls, instead of being given any preparation for living alone or being encouraged to discover who we were, many of us were taught to do nothing but look pretty and wait for Prince Charming to come along. In essence, we were taught to defer the development of our personalities until we found a man.

People with low self-esteem often have a difficult time accepting their aloneness. In their desperate search for completion they will look to anyone or anything—except themselves. In his book *The Psychology of Romantic Love,* Nathaniel Branden states:

> Aloneness entails self-responsibility. No one can think for us, no one can feel for us, no one can live our life for us, and no one can give meaning to our existence except ourselves. For most people, this fact is terrifying. It may be the most fiercely resisted, the most passionately denied, fact of their being.
>
> The forms their denial take are endless: refusing to think and following uncritically the beliefs of others; disowning one's deepest feelings in order to "belong"; pretending to be helpless, pretending to be confused, pretending to be stupid, in order to avoid taking an independent stand; clinging to the belief that one will "die" if one does not have the love of this person or that; joining mass movements or "causes" that promise to spare one the responsibility of independent judgment and to obviate the need for a sense of personal identity; surrendering one's mind to a leader; killing and dying for symbols and abstractions that promise to grant glory and meaning to one's existence, with no effort required on one's own part save obedience; devoting all of one's energies to manipulating people into giving "love."

Being totally honest with ourselves is extremely difficult. But without complete honesty, there is no real sense of self. I sometimes suggest to my clients that they start a "truth book," in which they commit to writing only the truth. Or, I suggest they make a commitment to writing only the truth when they write in their journals from now on. One of my clients, Virginia, had a very difficult time with this:

> I did as you suggested and started a truth book. But I haven't been able to write anything in it. I start to write something down, and then I realize it is a lie or an exaggeration, or that I have changed the truth somehow—softened it, stretched it, made it easier to swallow. I realize that I don't even know what the truth is. I've pretended so long, made myself into what others wanted for so long, hid from myself so long, that I have lost the truth, just like I lost myself.

I encouraged Virginia to continue trying, and I commended her for being willing to be so brutally honest with herself. I suggested that she did, indeed, have some truths to put in her truth book: she could write that she didn't know what the truth was, and that she has pretended so long that she has lost the truth. I could see the excitement in her eyes as she said, "That's right—I can write about what I just told you!" Virginia was doing what very few people ever have the nerve to do, and I knew that if she continued she was going to find herself.

In her book *An Unknown Woman: A Journey of Self-Discovery*, Alice Koller writes of the three months she spent alone in the middle of winter on the island of Nantucket, thirty miles off the Massachusetts coast. Koller went to Nantucket to find herself and to face all that she had fled from throughout her thirty-seven years. Alone, she begins to face the truth about herself:

> But think of all the ways there are to lie, and I'll have done every one of them. Pretending to like something because someone in authority does. Evading a question. Saying only part of what I believe. Not saying anything at all. Shaping my words to fit what I know will be acceptable. Smiling when someone intends to be funny. Looking serious when my thoughts are elsewhere. Agreeing when I haven't even thought over the matter. Drawing someone out just because I know he wants to talk. Trying to amuse in order to avoid talking about something I'm not sure of.
>
> Acting. For the dear love of God, how could I not have understood it before! Those are all pieces of acting. And I don't know where it ends. I have to try to think of one thing I've done that was for free.

Like Alice Koller and my client Virginia, you may have pretended to be someone else for so long that you have nearly lost yourself.

YOUR JOURNEY TOWARD SELF-DISCOVERY

Because all your life people have been telling you who you are and what your motivations are for doing the things you do, because you have lost yourself in your attempts to please others, because you've tried to be what you thought others expected you to be, you haven't had a chance to discover exactly who you really are.

Now is the time. There is absolutely nothing as important as taking this time out for self-discovery. There are a number of ways that you can begin your journey toward self-discovery. The most ideal way of doing this is to begin to spend extended periods of time alone. Begin with just fifteen minutes at a time and work your way up to an hour. Eventually, you'll be able to spend a whole day alone. Some of you may even be able to go away for a weekend all alone to a cabin in the mountains or a house by the beach.

Set up your time alone so that you are not distracted by telephone calls or other interruptions. If you have children it will be harder to get your time alone, but it is not impossible. Arrange to baby-sit a friend's children in exchange for her taking your children to her house for a few hours or even overnight. Have total silence, if at all possible. This means no radio or television during your alone time.

You will need to spend your time alone concentrating only on yourself—your feelings, your awarenesses, your thoughts, and your body. One of the best ways to discover who you are is to focus on what you feel. Only by getting to know yourself through your emotions can you grow to truly trust yourself and your perceptions.

It can be extremely difficult to focus this much attention on yourself and on your feelings. Most people have a very hard time spending even a few minutes focusing in this way. You may become extremely nervous and agitated, and you may find all kinds of ways to distract yourself from yourself. Don't be critical of yourself if you can't spend much time alone at first. If you stick with it and try just a few minutes at a time, you'll gradually be able to work your way up to an hour at a time.

An integral part of your self is the particular emotion you are feeling at any given moment. Begin each day by "checking in" with yourself. (Often, we are most open and vulnerable early in the morning, before we have put up any walls in order to face the world.) Sit quietly and breathe deeply. Ask yourself the following questions:

☐ How am I feeling right now?
☐ What is the emotion I am feeling?
☐ Why am I feeling this emotion? What caused it?

Perhaps a dream caused you to wake up feeling a particular emotion, since we often express in our dreams feelings that we are afraid to confront when we are awake. To help you to discover how you are feeling, pay particular attention to how your body feels. Do you have any tension or pain? If so, do you know what is causing the discomfort? What emotion do you associate with the discomfort? Fear? Anger? Sadness? Getting in touch with your body will also help you to get in touch with your emotions. Each time you deny a feeling, you deny a part of your *self.* Acknowledge and express your fear, your hurt, your anger, and your joy. Don't be alarmed if you experience a lot of intense emotions that you didn't know you had. Just allow the feelings to emerge, comfort yourself and your inner child, and see the experience as a healing one.

Try to check in with yourself several times a day. As an aid to self-discovery, I suggest that you start a journal. In your journal you can record your feelings, innermost thoughts, and dreams. Writing in your journal will help you to stay focused and will provide you with an outlet for self-expression. You will likely discover more about yourself than you ever imagined possible. You will discover thoughts and feelings long buried, solutions and alternatives to problem situations, new ways of looking at things, and—most important—new ways of looking at yourself.

Alice Koller describes the purpose and method of her inner journey:

> I'm here to understand myself, deliberately to turn myself open to my own view. I know, as I sit here, what I must have known for many years, that I can recognize what's true about myself when I see it. It's whatever I find myself refusing to admit, whatever I say no to very fast. That blanket admission right at the start may save me a lot of time. May save me, period. I'm using that "no" to protect myself from something. What? I'll find out. I'll write down everything I can remember, so that I can see the full extent of it, pick out some patterns in what I've been denying for so long.
>
> So that's first: to get it all written, no matter how ugly.

You may want to structure your journal-writing in a similar way. Writing down the story of your life, especially if you allow yourself to reexperience your emotions all along the way, can certainly be enlightening. But you need not do anything so formal or structured. Simply writing down your feelings at the moment can be very revealing.

Even if you spend only an hour a day for the purpose of honest self-discovery, you will slowly begin to know yourself in a way you may have never thought possible. You can spend your hour in silence, in meditation, writing in your journal, or just feeling.

If you find that you are not disciplined enough to set aside an hour a day for yourself, this may be a good time for you to enter psychotherapy. Making a commitment to attend a therapy session once a week may be the only way you can put this time aside. Then perhaps you can extend the time to the hour before therapy in order to prepare yourself for your session, or to the hour after therapy so you can absorb the insights from your therapy session. Another way to structure your time so that you are committed to self-discovery might be to schedule a body massage once a week, if you can afford it. This will provide you with a quiet time to feel your emotions and just focus on you. This is especially beneficial if you dedicate the hour after your massage to sitting quietly, allowing feelings and thoughts to emerge and writing down your feelings in your journal. Taking a walk early in the morning or in the evening can also give you the opportunity to be alone with your thoughts and feelings.

GETTING TO KNOW YOURSELF

Many women, having invested all their time and energy in attracting and pleasing a man, have very little self-knowledge. Without sufficient knowledge of who they are, they feel they have no true self, and they lack self-esteem. They are like the selfless women described earlier in this book, who see themselves as having little self at all or experience that self as being full of holes. Having virtually no awareness of self, they have nothing to like or value. It stands to reason that women who see themselves as a blank have virtually no chance of experiencing self-esteem.

Take some time to do a self-inventory or self-analysis. The following exercise can help you to become better acquainted with yourself.

Write a description of yourself, confining your description to your personality characteristics. (Exclude your physical characteristics and other "demographic" facts, such as your occupation, etc.) This may take you quite some time, because you may think you do not know enough about yourself at this point to write about. If you feel stuck, use the questions that follow, here and on the next pages, as a guide.

☐ What do I like about myself?

☐ What do I like best/least about myself?

☐ How do I feel about my body?

☐ How do I like to spend my leisure time?

   You may be very surprised to discover that this particular question really takes some conscious thought and experimentation. You have probably been so involved in pleasing others that you may not know what actually pleases you. If you seldom or never make suggestions as to where to go for entertainment, for example, you may discover that you actually don't know what you like in the way of movies, music, art, or sports. Because you are so compromising and complacent and tend to just "go along," you may have convinced yourself that you are easygoing and that, for example, you like all kinds of music—only to discover that there are some types of music that you actually hate. Or, you may have become so influenced by what other people like that you have lost track of what *you* like.

   Many emotionally abused women remain so busy either taking care of others' needs or obsessively working that they have very little leisure time. This is not an accident, of course. Sometimes we stay busy in order to avoid time alone. In addition, some women focus too much of their attention on men because they haven't found enjoyable ways of spending their leisure time. Selfless women, in particular, find that they are bored when they are alone and wander aimlessly around the house longing for someone to call or come by.

One of the most constructive and fulfilling ways of spending your leisure time is to find some way of expressing yourself creatively. Expressing yourself through art, music, or writing can help you to develop a stronger sense of self through creative expression of your emotions.

Another constructive way of spending your leisure time is sports, dance, or other body movement since the more you move your body the more you can get in touch with your emotions and your self.

☐ What kinds of people do I prefer to be around?

Because you've been led around by your negative patterns and your unfinished business, you have had little opportunity to discover what kinds of people you actually prefer to be around and are most comfortable with. (Note that *comfortable* here does not mean simply familiarity, but rather a feeling of being comfortable in your body, relaxed, happy, and at ease.)

Begin to notice how you feel when you are with different people. Which of your friends or relatives do you feel most at ease with? With whom do you feel stimulated and interested, and with whom do you feel bored?

This exercise can help you determine the kind of person you like:

1. Make a list of the qualities you most value in another person.
2. Make a list of the qualities you like least in another person.

☐ What kind of work is most fulfilling for me?

Surprisingly, even your choice of profession can be influenced by your unfinished business. In an attempt to please a parent, you may have chosen to go into a profession that you are really ill-suited for. Or, as a way of rebelling against your parents' insistence that you go into a certain kind of work, you may have steered clear of it, even though you actually would have enjoyed it.

Emotionally abused women are often drawn toward the helping professions because they want to give what they never got, or because they learned in life that helping others was the only way they could get any approval. Once you begin to get healthier and begin to heal from the emotional abuse you sustained as a child, you may discover that you really don't like this kind of work after all.

On the other hand, you may have never really decided what kind of career you want, but instead may have taken any job that came along, or you may have gone directly from high school into marriage and raising children.

The things you will discover about yourself may be exciting but also scary. It is important to realize that just because you have discovered something new about yourself doesn't mean you have to act on this new information right away. For example, if you realize that you are unhappy in the career that you are in, you don't have to quit your job right now and look for another one. Give yourself time to absorb this new information before you make any drastic changes in your life. You can learn all kinds of things from observing yourself, noticing how you feel, what you prefer, when you are comfortable, and when you are not. Since I started self-observing, I am often surprised at what I learn about myself every day. For example, the other day I was eating breakfast in my sunny dining room with the French doors open to the patio. As I sat looking out at my flowers, a slight breeze blew in. All of a sudden I was overtaken by a desire to go outside so I could feel the breeze on my face. I told myself to finish breakfast first. But the idea of feeling the breeze on my face gave me such a delicious feeling that I decided to go outside right away. It felt wonderful.

I learned several things about myself from this simple experience:

I love the cool ocean breeze so much that I always want to live close enough to the ocean to feel it.

I seldom act on my impulses to enjoy nature or something sensual if I have another task I am focusing on.

I often deny myself the things that feel good because my parental voice says I should do something else first.

Begin to feel what it is like to do what *you* want to do. Learn what you like and dislike so that you can begin to make choices based on your real desires, perhaps for the first time. Learn that you don't have to live your life based on what others want you to do, or on what you think you *should* do. Begin to get rid of habits and beliefs and ways of thinking that aren't genuinely yours, that have been imposed on you from outside.

LEARNING TO BE RESPONSIBLE FOR YOURSELF

As hard as it is to fully acknowledge, we do, indeed, come into the world alone, die alone, and essentially live all the days in between alone. That doesn't mean we cannot share some very meaningful, fulfilling, and intimate times with those we love along the way, but it does mean that we are the only constant, the only person we can rely on to be there for ourselves *no matter what.*

Unfortunately, all too often we let ourselves down by not taking care of ourselves, by ignoring our true wishes and desires, and by subjugating our needs to the needs of others. We must begin meeting our own needs, understanding once and for all that no one else is going to take responsibility for us or take care of us. As unbearable as it may seem, we must learn to take care of ourselves.

Rosemary, a client of mine who had just left a disastrous marriage to a man she had known for only three weeks when she married him, came to the conclusion that she had been operating in a fantasy world, always looking for someone to come along who would take care of her.

I got fooled by Joe because he was so good to me when I first met him. He treated me like a princess, and I loved it. I was sick of working and had been fantasizing about meeting a man who would support me, and Joe insisted that I quit my job as soon as we got married. What a dream come true! Joe took care of everything. He cooked, cleaned, and waited on me hand and foot.

But it wasn't long before my dream turned into a nightmare. Joe became very possessive, wanting me to spend all my time with him, wanting me to stop seeing my friends and family and insisting that he go everywhere I went. I began to feel like a caged bird. Whenever I tried to have a life of my own he would become irate, yelling and screaming at me that I was an ungrateful bitch, that I just married him for his money, and that I was a lazy slob.

I realize now that nothing comes easily, and that there are no free rides. I set myself up to be abused by Joe by giving myself over to him so freely, by wanting someone to take care of me. He took care of me all right, but the price was too high to pay.

Alice Koller wrote the following after spending some time alone:

Six days ago. And all I know so far is that color is important to me and that a lot of people have tried for a lot of years to make me responsible for my own life. But I seem to find that responsibility unendurable, like being underwater without enough air. And whenever I can find some way to break that pressure, I come up for air, screaming. Like a baby at its first gasp. And then, as if propelled by what I've just inhaled, I skitter in an almost random direction until the burst of energy gives out. And then I light, again at random, and stay, for almost no reason, until I sink below the surface. And then I do the whole thing over again.

The price we pay for flitting about from relationship to relationship, frantically looking for someone to take responsibility for us, is that parts of us get scattered all over the place and we lose ourselves. The price we pay for not shouldering our own burdens is that we eventually lose the strength to hold ourselves up.

If you are not willing to trust yourself, other people and events will determine the direction of your life. Begin to listen to your own heart. Follow your passion, and trust your inner wisdom, even if this means giving up what is secure and familiar. Be true to yourself, even if it means losing the approval of others and risking rejection. Be willing to give up what you think you should feel, do, or think in exchange for being who you really are. Your inner wisdom will blossom only if you give yourself time and space alone.

Raising Your Self-Esteem

Nothing is as important to our psychological well-being as our self-esteem. Our level of self-esteem affects virtually every aspect of our lives. It affects how we perceive ourselves and others, and it affects how others perceive us. It affects all our choices in life, from what career we choose to whom we choose to get involved with. It affects our ability to both give and receive love and our ability to take action when things need to be changed. It affects our ability to be creative. It affects our stability, and it even affects whether we are followers or leaders.

Self-esteem is how a person feels about herself; it is her overall judgment of herself. Our self-esteem may be high or low, depending on how much we like and approve of ourselves. If we have high self-esteem, we have an appreciation of the full extent of our personality. This means that we accept ourselves for who we are, with both our good qualities and our so-called bad ones. If we have high self-esteem, it can be assumed that we have self-respect, self-love, and feelings of self-worth.

As sad as it is, many women do not like themselves. They are plagued with gnawing doubts about their abilities and worth, or they actually feel worthless.

Many people use the words *self-esteem* and *self-concept* interchangeably, but these really have different meanings. Our self-concept, or self-image, is the set of beliefs and images we have about ourselves. Our self-esteem is the measure of how much we like and approve of our self-concept.

Our self-concept is made up of a wide variety of images and beliefs. Some of these are self-evident and easily verifiable (for example, "I am a woman," "I am a teacher," "I am a mother"). But there are also other, less tangible aspects of the self (for example, "I am intelligent," "I am incompetent," "I am worthless").

Many of the ideas we have about ourselves were acquired in childhood, from two sources: how others treated us, and what others told us about ourselves. How others saw us has thus become how we now see ourselves. Your self-concept—who you think you are—is a package that you have put together from how others have seen and treated you, and from the conclusions you drew in comparing yourself to others.

SIFTING THROUGH PARENTAL MESSAGES

As a child, you were repeatedly bombarded with messages from your parents about who you were. Sometimes these messages were spoken, and sometimes they were unspoken (for example, facial expressions, touch, body movements, and tone of voice).

As infants, if we are held close and comforted, if our mother notices our every movement and delights in our reactions, we feel loved and valued. If, on the other hand, our mother is indifferent to us, if her attention is not on our movements and reactions but elsewhere, we feel as if we are not important, not worth her attention.

Later on, if our parents tell us that we are pretty, smart, and lovable, the chances are very high that we will develop a positive self-image. However, if our parents tell us that we are ugly, stupid, and selfish, the reverse will likely occur. Since as children we respect and admire our parents, we believe that what they say is true, and our self-image plummets.

Self-discovery involves realizing who you are *not* almost as much as realizing who you *are*. Just as you are not your parents, you are also not necessarily who they have said you are. To learn what messages you absorbed about yourself as a child, do the following exercise:

1. Write down all the negative messages you received about yourself from your parents and family of origin.
2. Being as objective and as honest as you can, decide which messages are true and which are false.
3. Cross out all the negative messages on the list that were not true or are no longer true, or that you no longer believe.
4. Circle those messages that you still believe to be true.

Of the messages on the list that you believe are still true today, which are really *negative* things about you? For example, Rachel's parents told her that she was stubborn and pigheaded, and she believes that this is true of her today. But what her parents called "stubbornness" was Rachel's unwillingness to allow them to run her life. In Rachel's case, this trait can best be described as assertiveness.

In addition, before you decide that a negative message is true, consult someone whose opinion you value greatly. Or, better yet, ask several people. Sometimes we are so "brainwashed" into believing we are bad that we see ourselves with a too-critical eye. We need some objective input to determine the accuracy of the message.

Sift through all the beliefs and messages you were given by your parents and significant others, and decide which you will keep and which you will throw away. It is likely that not *all* of your parents' ideas, beliefs, and values were false or dysfunctional. Some may have been practical and valuable. You will need to decide for yourself which are true for you.

In addition, each of us learned strong ideas about who we should be and what we should be like. Girls often reach less of their potential than boys, often because their mothers were never taught to value themselves and thus had little or no sense of their own worth, power, or self. These women in turn passed on to their daughters a profound sense of inferiority. Whereas our ideas about who we actually are make up our self-concept, or perceived self, our ideas about who we *should* be form our ideal self. Most of us constantly compare our perceived self to our ideal self. The wider the gap between the two, the lower our level of self-esteem.

WHAT CAN YOU DO TO BEGIN RAISING YOUR SELF-ESTEEM?

Beyond a doubt, the most important thing you can do to raise your self-esteem is to stop being so critical of yourself. Your low opinion of yourself was caused to a great extent by others having been critical of you in the first place. Our self-esteem is chipped away by parents, siblings, schoolmates, friends, lovers, and bosses. From being criticized by others you developed a lifelong pattern of being self-critical, which in turn has constantly reinforced your low self-esteem.

Notice How Often You Are Self-Critical

You cannot stop this lifelong pattern overnight, but you can at least begin to notice how often you are self-critical—which may, by the way, be constantly. Many of my clients have been amazed at how often they find themselves being self-critical once they have begun to pay attention to it:

> I was actually shocked to realize how often I am critical of myself. I put myself down whenever I make even the slightest mistake. If I spill some coffee, I berate myself. If I am a few minutes late, I reprimand myself. I really don't let myself get away with anything. I guess I really expect myself to be perfect.

> No wonder I feel so bad about myself—I berate myself constantly! I can't do anything right, as far as I am concerned. Even if I am praised by other people for a job I've done, I can still find something wrong with it.

> I've noticed that I hear this little critical voice inside my head throughout the day, chastising me, scolding me, telling me that I'm wrong to do what I'm doing. It's a wonder I get anything done, considering the fact that I have this internal critic jabbering at me all the time!

Constant self-criticism makes you feel terrible about yourself. When you are being self-critical, you are doing the same thing to yourself that your parents and other original abusers did to you—you are damaging your self-esteem.

Like the last client above, you probably have a critical voice inside your head. That voice is most likely the voice of one of your parents or another original abuser. Unconsciously, through a process called *introjection,* you took that critical voice and made it your own. Some people call this process "becoming your own critical parent." You can hear this critical voice throughout the day, especially when you make a mistake.

You may want to begin writing down what your critical voice says to you. Not surprisingly, you may discover that you are saying to yourself the exact words that one of your parents said to you when you were a child—for instance:

"Can't you do anything right?"

"I can't believe you just did that—what an idiot!"

"How could you make such a stupid mistake? Where's your head?"

"What's wrong with you? You're not even trying!"

Pay attention to your self-talk or inner dialogues. Try to catch yourself whenever you engage in a critical, negative thought about yourself, and *stop it*! Ask yourself whose voice you are hearing—your own? Or one of your abusers? Try to remember whether someone from your childhood used to talk to you like that. Counter the message with something like, "That's not true! I am *not* stupid. I just made a mistake." Then work on replacing your negative self-talk with positive, encouraging statements, such as "I am really working on myself" or "I am doing the best I can."

Begin to Give Yourself More Praise

In addition to noticing how often you are self-critical, notice how often you are self-praising. Self-criticism is damaging in itself, but when coupled with a lack of self-praise it can be devastating. Not only were you probably overcriticized when you were a child, but you were probably seldom praised.

The regular use of self-praise builds self-confidence and validates your real worth. Talk to yourself lovingly, approvingly, reassuringly. Resist the temptation to be self-effacing or self-critical, even when you are not totally satisfied with your performance. Consistently give yourself praise, recognizing the good you have accomplished, just as a nurturing parent would. Support yourself with statements like "Hey, look how well you handled that!" or "I believe in you—I know you can do it." Not only is it important for you to say these things to yourself, it is important to really *absorb* them.

Tammy, a client of mine who suffers from very low self-esteem, told me: "My parents never praised me when I was a child. All they did was point out my mistakes and focus on what was wrong with me. I grew up thinking there was nothing good about me and feeling like there was no reason to even try."

Although you cannot stop criticizing yourself right away and may never stop entirely, always try to balance your self-criticism with self-praise.

1. Make a list of all your "negative" qualities, all your shortcomings and weaknesses, and all the things you do not like about yourself.
2. Now list all your strengths, positive attributes, and things you like about yourself.

Notice which list is longer. If your list of negatives is longer than your list of positives, you may tend to focus more on your liabilities than on your assets. Perhaps you take your strengths and positive attributes for granted, concentrating instead on your weaknesses. You probably have had a lot more practice finding the negatives because that is what your parents practiced with you.

Give yourself permission to see what is right with you. Since you probably have a great need for fairness, be fair with yourself by focusing on your assets at least as often as you do your liabilities. You don't have to sweep your weaknesses under the carpet, but try to balance them with your positives.

Ask a supportive friend who knows you well for help in adding to your list of positives. Carry this list with you so that you can add to it whenever you think of something new or when someone gives you praise. Continue this process until your strengths list is at least as long as your weaknesses list.

Read over your strengths list at least once a week. As you go over each strength, take a deep breath and absorb the knowledge that you possess this positive quality. It is difficult to hold on to your negative self-image if you let in evidence of your positive attributes.

Focus on Your Positive Attributes, Not on Your Flaws

Many women push their positive attributes to the side and instead focus on what they perceive as their flaws, no matter how small, to the point at which they begin to totally identify with those flaws. For example, instead of seeing yourself as a woman who is bright, talented, and funny but who also happens to be overweight, you identify yourself only as being overweight.

Begin to focus on your good qualities instead of on your negative ones.

Complete the following sentence until you have at least ten responses:

I like myself because _____ .

Examples:

I like myself because I continue to work on my personal issues.

I like myself because I am willing to admit when I have made a mistake.

I like myself because I try not to judge others harshly.

Refer to your list often. Ask those you are close to what they like about you, and add it to your list.

Work on Self-Acceptance

Very little of what makes you who you are today was under your control. You had no say as to what genes you would inherit, who your parents were, or how they were going to treat you.

And, most certainly, the emotional abuse you sustained as a child was not under your control. Your parents emotionally abused you because they were treating you the way they had been treated as children or because they had low self-esteem themselves. They were cruel, angry, neglectful, indifferent, and controlling because of their own problems. You did not cause these problems, nor did you cause your parents to be abusive to you by any of your actions.

It is crucial that you recognize that your low self-esteem, your tendency to get involved with abusive people, and all the other symptoms of your having been emotionally abused as a child are not your fault and were beyond your control up until now. This is a big step toward learning to accept yourself for who you are today.

Instead of judging yourself harshly for your shortcomings, try giving yourself the same benefit of the doubt that you probably give others when they aren't perfect. Try giving yourself half as much understanding as you have given all the abusive people in your life. When others have been emotionally abusive to you, how have you handled it in the past? Did you immediately try to make excuses for their behavior? Did you try to convince yourself that they really didn't mean to hurt you or that they were probably upset about something else? If you are like most emotionally abused women you have probably used all these rationalizations and more to excuse another person's abusive behavior. I'm not encouraging you to rationalize your behavior, but I do want you to try to understand why you are the way you are and recognize that until now you haven't known of a way to change yourself.

Raising your self-esteem means learning to accept who you already are rather than trying to change who you are or trying to create a whole new you.

Set Reachable Goals

Some women set impossibly high standards for themselves. They expect themselves to be perfect, and they are extremely self-critical when they make mistakes or don't meet their own unreasonably high expectations. If you are one of these women, be aware that this self-criticism is very damaging to your self-esteem and is preventing you from ever feeling the satisfaction of experiencing success, which can raise self-esteem.

If you are overweight, a reachable goal might be to lose thirty pounds. An unreachable goal might be to become a size six again, as you were at 18. While it may not be an impossible goal, to have such a high expectation of yourself when you are just starting to diet can easily cause you to become discouraged.

We all need the experience of success to raise our self-esteem. But to feel successful we need to set goals that are reachable. Don't set goals that are so outrageous that you will only be setting yourself up for failure.

Stop Taking Things So Personally

Because you were so severely criticized as a child, and because you were often blamed for whatever went wrong in your parents' lives, you may be hypersensitive to criticism and judgments from others. For example, when a store clerk is rude, instead of either getting angry and insisting on being treated courteously or assuming that the clerk is just having a bad day, you may take it as a reflection of your own worth. You may wonder, "Did I do something to irritate her?"—thus taking responsibility for something that probably has nothing to do with you. If someone happens to mention that you look tired, rather than hearing it as an expression of concern, you may assume that the person is voicing doubts about your ability to function or is trying to tell you that you look old. While once in a while this may be the case, usually the other person is just expressing concern. If you assume that every truly innocent comment means that there is something wrong with you or that you are being criticized, such incidents can cause you to feel completely worthless or to adamantly defend yourself against a nonexistent attack.

Try to take things at face value instead of assuming there is hidden meaning in every statement. If someone says something that causes you to doubt yourself or his intention, ask him to clarify what he meant by the comment. If it was an innocent statement, he will be happy to explain exactly what he meant.

Stop Mind Reading

Because you are so convinced that you are worthless, flawed, or inadequate, you may assume that others see you that way too. This belief may cause you to have a tendency to "mind read"— that is, to assume that you know what others are really thinking.

Judging you is not the foremost priority in everyone else's life. When you are assuming that others are thinking bad thoughts about you, they probably aren't even thinking about you at all.

If someone seems upset, don't assume it is because of you or something you've done. Check out your perceptions by asking the person, "What's going on with you?" or "How are you feeling?"

Stop Letting Others Define You

Because of your low self-esteem, you may tend to be excessively concerned about what other people think of you. When someone is critical of a specific behavior of yours, you may take it as a criticism of your entire person—as an attack on your overall worth—causing your self-esteem to crumble in an instant.

Besides allowing negative responses from others to ruin your day, you may also allow a positive response from someone to "make" your day. However, this gives other people way too much control over how you feel about yourself and makes you vulnerable to insincere flattery and manipulation.

Hilary's boss can easily manipulate her by complimenting her on her work when he wants her to do something extra for him and by criticizing her work when she doesn't comply. Since she has little sense of whether she is a good worker aside from her boss's feedback, she either thinks she is the greatest employee around or the worst. As long as she depends upon the boss's comments for her sense of herself as a worker, Hilary will continue to be manipulated by him. She needs instead to have reasonable expectations of herself and to work on praising herself and giving herself positive "self-talk" whenever she completes a task.

Stop Comparing Yourself with Others

You have probably been comparing yourself to others ever since you were a little girl looking around at other families and noticing that other parents seemed to love, approve of, and encourage their children a lot more than yours did. You may have hung around other children's homes a lot, trying to absorb a lifestyle that was more desirable than yours. Being on the outside looking in is a familiar feeling for emotionally abused children.

Many emotionally abused women spend a great deal of time and energy figuring out how they rate in comparison to those around them. Because they have no sense of inherent worth, their level of self-esteem fluctuates wildly, depending upon whether they see themselves as better or worse than their "competitors." Obviously, it is impossible not to compare ourselves with others at times; in fact, we gain a great deal of information about ourselves and how we fit into the world by looking at ourselves in comparison to others. But comparisons are not beneficial when they become habitual. Constantly comparing yourself to everyone you encounter can cause you to feel extremely bad about yourself, because you can always find someone who is younger, prettier, thinner, richer, or more successful. When we habitually compare ourselves to others we are likely to end up seeing ourselves as inferior and constantly feeling envious.

The next time you start to compare yourself to someone, try telling yourself that she is just *different* from you, without placing a judgment value on how she is different. Even if that person seems to have more than you do or be more accomplished than you, remind yourself that this doesn't mean she is better than you or has more worth than you. Other people's successes or failures are not reflections of our worth. Instead of saying to yourself, "She's so lucky to have that guy—I'll never get someone like that" or "How did *she* get a guy like that?" try telling yourself, "I hope I can be as happy with someone someday as she seems to be with that guy."

Also, remember that when we envy someone we are usually seeing an incomplete picture. If we view others from a realistic perspective and not from an idealized one, we will recognize that it does, indeed, all balance out. No one has everything, and, in fact, many people probably admire you for your attributes. Bolster your self-esteem by turning your attention to your own good qualities.

Just as pining away for what others had made you feel even worse when you were a child, it will continue to make you feel deprived and inadequate today. Remind yourself that you have a lot more options today than you did as a child. Instead of envying what others have, decide what *you* want out of life, and go after it.

Stop Seeing Yourself in All-or-Nothing Terms

When you assess yourself in all-or-nothing terms, you see yourself as either extremely competent or totally incompetent, as a total success or a miserable failure.

Stop exaggerating the severity of your flaws. When we exaggerate our flaws, those of us who are only slightly overweight see ourselves as grossly obese; those who have short tempers view ourselves as explosive bitches; those who are occasionally slow in catching on to new ideas see ourselves as stupid.

Remember that no aspect of ourselves, no matter how much we like it or dislike it, represents the whole of us. The following exercise can help you to see yourself in perspective instead of identifying yourself in terms of only one attribute or aspect of yourself.

For each attribute, aspect, or description of yourself, complete the following sentence:

My _____ is a part of me; I am not my _____ .

Examples:

My intellect is a part of me; I am not my intellect.

My body is a part of me; I am not my body.

My stuttering is a part of me; I am not my stuttering.

Do this exercise whenever you begin to focus on one or two negative aspects of yourself and begin to feel worthless as a result. Seeing a flaw as only one part of who you are instead of as the whole of you will help you to accept that aspect of yourself and free you to change it, if possible.

Accept That You, and Others, Are Both Good and Bad

Because we don't allow ourselves to be imperfect, because we feel so bad and guilty for making mistakes, we work very hard at being "good." We must *always* be fair and right, always patient, diligent, and understanding. We alternate between excessive self-righteousness ("Why can't everyone be as good and fair as I am?") and excessive self-hatred ("No one is as bad or evil as I am"). Even though we work hard at being good, we usually feel bad.

We also see others as either all good or all bad. We idealize people, put them on pedestals, and trust them without testing them. Then, when they behave like normal, fallible human beings, we cast them out of our lives—"You aren't perfect. You have failed me. You're no good." When someone hurts us, disappoints us, or does something that seems unfair to us, we immediately see them as all bad. We lose all trust in them, and sometimes all love for them. At that moment we do not believe they have any redeeming qualities. We "forget" any good qualities we once thought they had, any good deeds they once did.

1. On a sheet of paper, make two columns by drawing a line down the center of the page. On one side of the paper list all your good qualities. In the other column, list all your bad qualities. Read the two lists, recognizing that they are *both* you, that you are made up of both good and bad qualities.
2. Make the same kind of list for each of your parents. Recognize that they, too, have both good and bad qualities.
3. List the good and bad qualities of other family members, fellow workers, friends, church leaders, and your favorite politicians or movie stars.

Begin Nurturing Yourself

Without a healthy image of yourself, you will not be motivated to practice healthier attitudes and behaviors. For this reason, you will need to begin to nurture yourself so that you can begin to love yourself for who you are.

Self-love is a healing force for recovery from emotional and physical wounds. The more you love yourself, the more you will be healed from the devastating damage caused by the emotional abuse to your mind, soul, and body. Caring for yourself, cherishing yourself, and treating yourself with tenderness—all the countless ways in which self-love is expressed—will contribute to your positive feelings about yourself, which in turn will help raise your self-esteem.

Here are three ways to express self-love:

1. Write your inner child a love letter. Tell her that you love her and why, listing all the wonderful characteristics she has that make her so lovable to you.
2. Write your adult self a love letter or a letter of recognition and admiration. Include all the things you love and admire about yourself, all the things you have accomplished, and all the progress you have made toward recovery. Encourage yourself to continue working and growing, and praise yourself for your courage.
3. Imagine that you have an identical twin who is actually a part of you. Place this "other you" in a chair facing you. With your eyes open or closed, "notice" clearly your coloring, features, and clothes. Tell yourself how deeply you care for this twin you, leaving no detail out in expressing all that she means to you. Spend as much time in your dialogue as you can. Then fantasize that the you on the chair merges into the you who is talking.

Take Care of Your Body

Self-nurturing also involves taking care of yourself physically. Many women who were emotionally abused and deprived are tremendously disrespectful of their bodies' needs. They tend to load their bodies with unhealthy food, alcohol, or drugs (including nicotine), drive themselves relentlessly, and refuse themselves adequate rest and tension-releasing exercise. This is understandable, of course, since we were never taught to respect and love our bodies. We probably learned instead to abuse our bodies by watching those around us abusing theirs through overeating, alcohol, and drugs or through neglect. As an adult, you have continued the pattern, and in your attempts to repress your uncomfortable emotions you may have abused your body even further.

Taking care of your body will be an important step toward gaining higher self-esteem. The following exercise can help you to make a stronger connection with your body:

1. Complete the sentence that follows, doing this as many times as necessary for you to have a better connection with how your body feels and what it is trying to tell you.

"I am your body, and I feel ＿＿＿＿＿＿＿＿＿＿＿＿＿＿＿＿ ."
Examples:

 I am your body, and I feel tired.

 I am your body, and I feel tense and angry.

 I am your body, and I feel like crying.

2. Addressing each part of your body separately, complete the following sentence:

"I am your ＿＿＿＿＿＿＿＿, and I feel ＿＿＿＿＿＿＿＿ ."
Examples:

 I am your arm, and I feel angry. I want to hit out! I want to push away the abuser! Let me hit and push!

 I am your heart, and I feel sad. I feel broken and wounded. I need you to help me mend. Give me some comforting and nurturing; I need your special care. Stop eating such fatty foods. It makes it hard for me to work.

3. Continue to tell your body, "I am going to make certain I feed you properly and that you get plenty of rest and exercise. I love you and want you to be healthy."

Do this complete exercise at least once a week. Your body will tell you what it needs. If you listen to it and give it the care it requires, you will be amazed at the increased self-love that will follow.

Promote Self-Healing

One of the best ways to promote self-healing is through touch. Even though you may be afraid of having someone else touch you because as a child you were physically and/or sexually abused or were so deprived of touch that it now makes you feel uncomfortable, being touched in a nonthreatening, nonsexual way can promote healing from the wounds of your childhood in a very profound way. Here are some of the ways you can begin receiving the healing of touch:

☐ Express affection by giving and receiving hugs.

☐ Get a manicure, pedicure, or facial.

☐ Get a massage from a qualified, licensed person, preferably someone of the same sex.

☐ Give yourself a massage.

☐ Have someone you love and trust hold you.

Allow the touch to remind you that your body is a wonderful creation, capable of bringing you pleasure as well as pain. Think beautiful, positive thoughts while you are being touched. Allow each touch to heal you of your wounds.

Before you can improve your relationships with others, you must first improve your relationship with yourself. How you feel about yourself directly affects how you live your life and how you relate to others. When your self-esteem is high, you will automatically treat those around you better.

It will take some time for you to change the lifelong habits and beliefs that have kept your self-esteem low, but the time you spend will be well worth the effort. Raising your self-esteem will help insure that you will never again put up with abusive behavior from anyone.

You deserve to be valued and treated with respect. Begin by treating yourself the way you want others to treat you.

CHAPTER 10

Changing Your Pattern and Breaking the Cycle of Abuse

"Nature has no use for the plea
that one 'did not know.' "

CARL JUNG

In the past, you may have tended to draw emotional abusers to you like bees to honey. As you let go more and more of your victim mentality, you will not find untrustworthy people so attractive, and, interestingly enough, they will also not find you attractive. Gaining insight into your particular pattern and making the connections between your past and your present have helped you to understand yourself and your motives better. However, because the unconscious drive to repeat the past is so compelling, you cannot expect yourself to change overnight. You will need to be vigilant so that you can short-circuit your old patterns as they reappear.

HOW TO CHANGE YOUR RELATIONSHIP PATTERN

Take Time to Get to Know People

All too often, we get involved with others before we have had a chance to really get to know them.

You cannot truly love someone you do not know. You can be in love with a fantasy or with who you *think* this person is, but you cannot be in love with the real person. Only over time, through observing the person in all kinds of situations and in all kinds of moods, can you truly learn about him.

The problem with "instant romance" is that by the time you finally get to know the person you have become involved with, you are already emotionally and sexually involved and can no longer be objective. As you have no doubt discovered, it is much more difficult to end a relationship once you are already invested in it.

Learn from your past mistakes. Get to know a new person slowly, whether it be a new friend or a new lover. You've been through a lot of pain already because you haven't taken your time in becoming involved in relationships. Don't give your heart away immediately, only to have it broken yet again.

Since you probably know the type of abuser you are likely to be attracted to, be on guard for this kind of person in particular. Even though you know your pattern, you will still find yourself drawn to the same abusive type. If you find yourself enormously attracted to someone right away, *beware!* This person is probably the same type of abusive person you have known all your life. If you feel as though you've known someone for years, it may be because in a sense you have known them for years. They are probably replicas of your original abuser(s). Protect your heart and protect your feelings by taking the time to find out *before* you become involved whether a person is a healthy choice for you as a friend or lover.

Continue Working on Setting Physical and Emotional Boundaries

When you were a child, abusers had easy access to you and were able to physically and/or sexually abuse you. Now, as an adult, you may behave as if you have no rights over your own body, allowing others to touch you when you do not want to be touched or even to physically abuse you.

You have the right to choose who can touch you and when, as well as what type of touch is acceptable to you. This does not refer to sexual touching only. If you do not like having your boss put his arm around you while he is talking to you, for example, you have the right to say something about it. Do it diplomatically at first, taking him aside and quietly telling him that it bothers you. But if he continues to do it, you have the right to tell him more firmly. *No one,* under *any* circumstances, has the right to touch you if you do not want to be touched! This includes doctors and nurses. If their touch is bothering you, ask them to do it differently.

You may also need to continue working on setting emotional boundaries. You may have allowed others to take over your life or otherwise control you, or you may have virtually "lost yourself" in others by becoming enmeshed in their lives. All of your energy and focus may have gone outward, toward others, so that you could anticipate and meet their needs.

Many women do a better job of taking care of themselves when they are not in a relationship. Before Rita met Robert, she was going to school at night. She told me, "I was exercising, and I was eating right. Now I drag myself home after work, too tired to go to school or to exercise. All I do is eat and take care of Robert's needs." This is a typical story. As soon as they become involved in a relationship, many women tend to stop doing those things that give them pleasure or a sense of accomplishment. Instead, they take on the task of pleasing their partners. It is no coincidence that many women gain weight when they are in a relationship. They do so not because they are so "content and happy," but because they have stopped taking care of themselves, meeting their own needs. They don't know how to have a relationship and maintain a sense of themselves at the same time.

While you may not have specific answers to the following questions, they will give you food for thought. By using these questions as a guide, you can begin to set emotional boundaries that are healthy for you.

- ☐ How much intimacy can I tolerate before I start to feel smothered?

- ☐ How much time can I spend with someone before I start to feel afraid or uncomfortable?

- ☐ How much can I share about myself before I feel I have shared too much?

Building Boundaries, Not Barricades

Out of fear of losing ourselves, we may build barricades instead of boundaries. To us, intimacy equals intrusion. We may become so fearful of giving ourselves up in love or in passion that we shut ourselves off from any experience of emotional surrender. We then become alienated from others and feel isolated, disconnected, and alone.

You will need to learn to distinguish between autonomy and alienation, connectedness and dependency. Ask yourself, "How far away can I go from another person and still feel connected?" and "How much am I willing to give up for love and security?" Everyone struggles with such questions from time to time, but those who were emotionally abused are constantly dealing with these conflicts when they are in relationships.

Curbing Your Urge to Merge

The flip side of the temptation to build barriers is the "urge to merge." Because they have difficulty in being aware of their own boundaries, many emotionally abused women also have difficulty respecting or even perceiving the boundaries of others. Laurie told me,

> I don't know how to have a relationship that isn't *intense*. There is no such thing as a casual relationship for me. I tell all. I share my deepest, darkest secrets and feelings, and I expect the other person to do the same. I force the intimacy. I don't know how to reach a middle ground in relationships. I'm either too intense, or I'm aloof and distant.

Those who were emotionally abused tend to "bare their souls" to others right away, very often as a way of capturing the other person's attention. In addition, those who were sexually abused as children may now operate on the assumption that the only way they can get a man to like them is to have sex with him. Learning to have nonsexual relationships or relationships that are more than just sexual is an important part of respecting and honoring your boundaries.

Try developing more balance in your life. Emotionally abused women tend to go to extremes. We are either celibate or we are promiscuous. We alternate between wanting to spend all our time with someone and not wanting to see this person at all. If your tendency is to spend all of your time with a new friend or lover, pull yourself away long enough to regain a sense of yourself. Then you won't be as likely to feel smothered by the relationship and have to distance yourself in the extreme ways that you have in the past.

Because you may have a tendency to become "lost" in another person and to become confused about the boundaries between yourself and others, try the following centering exercise after you have an intense exchange (whether it be a conversation, an intimate moment of touching and closeness, or a sexual experience).

☐ Sit alone quietly with your eyes closed.

☐ Start breathing deeply, imagining that with each inhale you are coming back into yourself.

Make Sure You're Not Just Afraid of Being Alone

In the past, you may have been so afraid of being alone that you would have done anything—and often did—to avoid it. When you were a child, your mother may have stayed with your father no matter what he did to you or to her out of her fear of being on her own. As an adult, you may have repeated the same pattern, clinging to destructive relationships in order to avoid being alone, staying in abusive situations (jobs, friendships, family and romantic relationships) out of fear of winding up alone.

Note, too, that all of us have particular times or circumstances when we are susceptible to getting involved with someone (for example, many people get lonely around the holidays and look for someone to spend the holidays with). Be aware of your own most susceptible times so that you can protect yourself.

Give Up Your Fantasy of the Knight on the White Horse

If you keep looking for someone to take care of you, you will continue to attract people who are overcontrolling and critical, and you will continue to be abused.

No one can rescue you or save you from yourself. You must begin to meet your own needs, relying on yourself for the nurturing you need.

How to Spot an Abuser

The following behaviors and personality characteristics are common among emotional abusers. These are warning signs, red flags, that the person may be more likely to be abusive. Not every abuser will have every characteristic, of course, but if the person you are considering getting involved with has many of these characteristics, you have reason to be concerned.

Poor impulse control

Low self-esteem

Selfishness and narcissism

Needy and demanding (of your time, attention, etc.)

Poor social skills; difficulties developing adult social and sexual relationships

Alcohol abuse; alcoholism or drug addiction

History of being abusive (physically, verbally, and sexually) as an adult or older child

History of mental illness

Dependent personality (unable to support self financially, emotionally)

Antisocial behavior (does not believe in society's rules, has own set of rules that seem to accommodate *his* desires)

Needs to feel powerful and in control

Aggressive, demanding, abusive

Preoccupied with sex; needs to have sex daily or several times a day; masturbates compulsively

BREAKING THE CYCLE: HOW TO AVOID BEING AN ABUSIVE PARENT

Even though they vowed they would not repeat the cycle of abuse, many women who were emotionally abused as children find that their worst nightmare has come true—they have become like their abusive parents and have abused their own children.

Others are afraid to have children because they are aware of their own tendency to be abusive. Still others long to have children and are determined not to make the same mistakes their parents did.

Those who were emotionally abused as children often end up abusing their own children in the very same ways that they were abused. Those who were verbally abused or overly criticized are often shocked to hear the same words out of their mouths that hurt them so much as children—"You're so stupid," "I wish I never had you," "I hate you." A mother who was ignored and deprived by her own parents will tend to neglect her children, while a mother who was smothered or overcontrolled will tend to repeat this particular behavior. Much to her dismay, Holly began to notice her own tendency to be abusive:

> I can't believe it. As hard as I've tried to not be like my mother, I've ended up just like her. When it comes to my kids, I sound just like her, I complain just like she did, and I expect too much from them, just as she did with me.

Those who were physically abused often become too rough with their children and find that they have to fight the urge to strike them. Or they may suddenly be gripped with rage at their children's impudence, and strike out uncontrollably.

The woman who was sexually abused as a child may be appalled at her own uncontrollable desire to touch her child sexually. She may go to the opposite extreme, depriving her child of touch and affection out of fear of being sexual with the child.

How can we stop this cycle of abuse? Knowing that we have a tendency to be abusive like our parents, how can we prevent ourselves from acting on these impulses?

Most emotionally abusive parenting is unintentional, a result of the inadequate personality development of the parents (who themselves did not have adequate role models). Parents may be the victims of their own parents' failures; they may also simply be unaware of the destructive consequences of their actions.

Parenting is an art and as such requires constant refinement and evaluation. It is naive to think that just by recognizing abusive patterns, parents can raise children who are completely healthy emotionally. Parents are human, and they are naturally going to make mistakes.

Don't Have Children for the Wrong Reasons

Abusive parents often have children for the wrong reasons. Having a child may be an effort to hold the marriage together, to feel loved and to satisfy loneliness, to fill a sense of emptiness, or to have someone to control. Abusive parents expect their children to fill their own emotional void. It is estimated that over 90 percent of child sexual abuse occurs in families where the parents have grossly unrealistic expectations of their children.

As a whole, parents who emotionally, physically, or sexually abuse their children are emotionally desperate and severely dependent, and they expect their children to make up for what they lack in their own lives. Instead of nurturing their children and meeting their emotional needs, parents who were deprived often wind up teaching their children to meet the parents' needs—as their parents did before them. Thus, the cycle perpetuates itself.

As a parent, you must not rely on your children to increase your low self-esteem. Parenting is not a popularity contest. Because you will need to provide your children with proper limits, boundaries, and discipline, there will be times when you will temporarily lose your children's affection. If you are not willing to adjust to this, you will bend to your child's wishes in an attempt to maintain his love, and you will risk turning your child into someone who always has to have his way. Parents with low self-esteem will tend to overinvest in their children, placing a tremendous burden on them to succeed.

Accept Your Children for Who They Are

Because many emotionally abused women are unable to experience self-esteem from within but instead attempt to gather it from outside, we are also unable to accept and appreciate our children solely for who they are. Instead, we praise them for their performance, their looks, their grades, and so on. Because we are basing our own self-esteem on our children's attributes and achievements, we make them feel ashamed of their mistakes and imperfections.

If we do not express our own emotions freely, we in turn have little ability to allow our children to have their feelings. While we are responsible for guiding them to healthy ways of thinking and acting, it is abusive to tell our children that they "can't" or "shouldn't" feel or think as they do. It is also abusive to make them feel ashamed of the way they look, dress, or behave. Instead, we need to confront what is inappropriate in a firm but supportive manner that respects the dignity of the child.

Children have a right to be listened to. Their ideas and opinions need to be respected. All too often, parents treat children as though they and their ideas are not important. To develop into independent, self-confident adults, children need to be encouraged to express themselves. Get to know your child. Accept her for who she is, not for who you want her to be.

Respect Your Children, and They Will Respect You

Abusive parents often demand total obedience from their children and demand their respect. However, respect is not automatically due you just because you are a parent, and you need to stop demanding it of your children. Your child will most likely show you respect if you respect *him*. The parent who displays no respect for her children can expect little respect in return.

If you were raised in a dysfunctional environment where boundaries and privacy were not respected, you probably do not have appropriate boundaries and do not respect your children's privacy. Out of your need to be in control or your fear that your child will do something wrong, you may be intrusive—going through your children's drawers, listening in on their telephone conversations, opening their mail. A child has a right to privacy, just as you do, and it is abusive to deny this right.

In addition, you need to teach your children to respect *your* privacy. You are not doing your child a favor by allowing her to intrude upon your space. Instead, you are teaching her to be intrusive with others and are discouraging her from developing a self that is separate from you. There are many ways that you can teach your children to respect your privacy and the privacy of others, and at the same time break the habit of being intrusive yourself. Among them are these:

☐ Close the door when you go to the bathroom, and stay out of the bathroom when your child is in there, even if the door is open.

☐ Do not read your children's mail, go through their private belongings, or listen to their private conversations.

☐ Respect your children's privacy by allowing them to close their bedroom doors and by not watching them bathe or use the toilet.

☐ Do not allow your children to sleep with you unless it is an unusual circumstance, and do not bathe or shower with them.

Provide Your Children with Proper Discipline and Limits

Many women who were emotionally or physically abused when they were children are so fearful of repeating the cycle and becoming abusive toward their own children, and so afraid of losing their children's love, that they don't set proper limits or administer proper discipline. As a result, their children may take advantage of their leniency by pushing their limits. In addition, children who are not given proper limits and rules will keep testing their parents' limits in an attempt to force them to draw the line.

Jill came to see me because she felt out of control with her children.

> I know I must be doing something wrong with my kids. They don't respect me at all. In fact, they treat me like I'm their slave. Instead of getting up and changing the television channel themselves, they order me to do it. They sit on the couch all night and tell me to get them a drink of water or a snack. The sad part about it is that I do it for them! I can't seem to be strong enough to tell them to do it them-selves. I know I am spoiling them, and I'm getting so I don't even like them, but I just can't bring myself to lay down the law.

As it turned out, because Jill's mother had been so emo-tionally abusive to her when she was a child, Jill was afraid of repeating the pattern and becoming abusive to her own kids. In addition, because her self-esteem has been so damaged, Jill was reluctant to stand up to anyone, even her own children.

Not only was Jill damaging herself by allowing her children to treat her this way, she was also insuring that her children would become immature adults who were unwilling to take care of their own needs. Children who are allowed to walk all over their parents will grow up to feel they are entitled to special treatment from others, will disrespect authority, and will lack proper limits and boundaries. As adults, they will continue to walk all over their parents and will even be emotionally abusive to them.

In his book *The Road Less Traveled*, psychiatrist M. Scott Peck stated,

> To fail to confront when confrontation is required for the nurture of spiritual growth represents a failure to love equally as much as does thoughtless criticism or condemnation and other forms of active de-privation of caring. If they love their children parents must, sparingly and carefully perhaps but nonetheless actively, confront and criticize them from time to time, just as they must also allow their children to

confront and criticize themselves in return. . . . Mutual, loving confrontation is a significant part of all successful and meaningful human relationships. Without it the relationship is either unsuccessful or shallow.

Encourage your children to take care of themselves and their possessions. If you do it all for them, they will never learn to do it themselves, as in the case of Kristin.

> My mother spoiled me completely. She did everything for me, including cleaning my room, doing my homework for me, and even washing my hair. Now, I can't seem to take care of myself. I neglect my health, my wardrobe, my bills. I lose or misplace my belongings, and my apartment is always a filthy mess. Worst of all, I keep choosing friends and lovers who want to help get me organized. Unfortunately, they end up controlling me and trying to run my life.

Do not overprotect your children. By constantly showing your child that you are afraid for her, you are giving her the message that life is dangerous and that to explore life's possibilities is to subject oneself to unnecessary risks. Allow your child to make her own mistakes. If you are not in a position to help your child in a specific situation, trust that she will be able to take care of herself.

Learn Appropriate Ways of Being Affectionate with Your Children

Children need to be held, nurtured, and comforted. Physical touch is so vital to their development that infants have been known to die from touch deprivation. Unfortunately, many adults who were abused as children have difficulty feeling comfortable with physical closeness and affection, not just with romantic partners but with anyone, including their own children. Touching and physical closeness do not come naturally to them, and they feel awkward about it. But because touch is so important, you will need to get past your own awkwardness and reticence, for your own sake as well as your children's.

Some of my clients have told me that they become afraid when their children get physically close to them. They fear having sexual feelings toward the child, or, in some cases, they believe or fear the child is being sexual with them. Because it is a confusing and difficult task to be able to distinguish between sexual feelings and love feelings, you may need to consult with a therapist about this issue. All parents are afraid of feeling sexual toward their children, and this is especially true for survivors of sexual abuse, as mentioned earlier. Talk about it in your support group, and write about your feelings. The important thing is that you continue to acknowledge your feelings and your fears. If you are very fearful of becoming sexual with your children or are afraid you will not be able to control yourself, or if you have begun to fantasize about sexual activity with your children and have even masturbated to these fantasies, *by all means seek professional help or attend a self-help group such as Parents United.*

If you have had no real thoughts or fantasies about sexually abusing your children and have come to realize that your fears are unwarranted and have to do with what happened to you, work on relaxing with your children and on *setting limits* as to where they can touch you and where you can touch them. You can begin to teach a child as young as five or six about private parts. If your child wants to touch your breasts, for example, explain to him that your breasts are your private parts and that you don't allow anyone else to touch them without your permission. Tell him that he should do the same thing with his body. Then distract the child by engaging him in another activity. Be aware that children are naturally affectionate and curious, and that your child is not being sexual with you just because he or she wants to touch your breasts.

Gwen told me how upset she was because her son kept trying to touch her breasts and "crawl all over me. I think he is being sexual with me!" she exclaimed. "I just can't take it. He's like an octopus—he has his hands everywhere." After several sessions of therapy, Gwen realized that her son was not being sexual with her at all, but just being a normal child. She was afraid of him because of her experience of childhood victimization. But she also found that even though she wanted to be close to her child, it was still difficult for her to let him "crawl all over" her.

Eventually, Gwen realized that her son was crawling all over her because she wasn't spending enough time with him. He was so needy for her that he was suffocating her. Once she started spending more time with him, telling him stories, and listening to him tell about his day at school, he no longer needed to grab on to her so much.

Give yourself permission to be *who you are now,* and forgive yourself for having some "hang-ups" about touching and closeness. You may never feel comfortable having your child sit on your lap or crawl all over you, but you can offer alternatives (such as sitting next to each other, giving lots of hugs, and holding hands). If you are affectionate, and your children know you love them, they will be okay.

Continue to Work on Yourself and on Being a Good Parent

Continue to work on your own unfinished business regarding your childhood abuse. Most abusive parents are still angry with their own abusive parents and are acting out this anger with their children. The more you work on releasing your anger in constructive ways, the less likely you will be to abuse your children.

Learn to recognize when your own inadequacies and weaknesses get in the way of your child's development. You can then rectify the situation by seeking help from psychotherapy or family counseling.

Your children also need you to protect them from other people who may be abusive to them. Continue to work on giving up your denial about your own childhood abuse. If you admit the truth about your family, you will not expose your child to those in the family who could abuse her. However, if you stay in denial, pretending that there was no abuse or that the person who abused you would never abuse your children, you will continue to pretend when your own child is being abused.

Learning to be a good parent is a continual process. There are numerous parenting classes now being offered at community colleges, and there are many fine books that teach parenting skills. One book that I recommend highly is called *Your Child's Self-Esteem,* by Dorothy Corkille Briggs. For those who find that they are becoming abusive I recommend individual therapy or a group called Parents Anonymous. Here you will meet other parents who have been abusive to their children, learn from them how they were able to stop, and learn effective parenting skills.

Breaking the cycle of abuse is a lifelong effort, both in terms of your not attracting abusive people into your life and of your not becoming abusive to your own children. Don't expect perfection. You will make many mistakes along the way. But if your intention is to break the cycle, and you are truly committed to not being abused or being abusive, you can be the person who breaks the cycle of abuse in your family.

Continuing to Change

The kinds of changes we have been talking about in this book—completing your unfinished business from the past, becoming more assertive, learning to walk away from abusive relationships, discovering yourself, raising your self-esteem, changing your pattern and breaking the cycle of abuse—all take time. None of these major tasks can be done in a short amount of time, because they all require major changes in your thinking, feeling, and behaving. Neither is there a prescribed amount of time required for each change. Some changes, such as becoming more assertive, may take a relatively short time; others, such as self-discovery, will take a lifetime.

With most of these changes there is no true beginning, middle, or end, but a continual progression toward our goals—a progression that sometimes falters, sometimes even halts altogether at times. There will even be times when you feel you have regressed, going backward instead of forward. But even at these times, be aware that you have regressed for a reason. For example, perhaps you have needed to revisit an old way of behaving one more time just to remind yourself of how bad it feels. Or, perhaps you have needed to go back one more time to an abusive person, just to remind yourself of how bad it feels to be negated, criticized, controlled, put down, or taken for granted.

When viewed in this light, regression can be seen as an inevitable, even positive aspect of change. Whatever you do, do not be critical of yourself for having to learn a lesson one more time. Often, the lessons we have learned the hard way are the ones that stick with us the most.

The kinds of changes we have been discussing in this book are actually major personality changes. Because your personality is pretty well set by the time you are an adult, changing it is an extremely difficult task. For those of you who have identified with what I call the "selfless woman," your changes will involve not just changing your personality but actually developing a personality that is reflective of who you really are.

SPECIFIC ADVICE FOR EACH TYPE OF EMOTIONALLY ABUSED WOMAN

Advice to the Selfless Woman

Because you were neglected, rejected, smothered, or overly criticized and controlled by your mother, you will more than likely continue to be attracted to people who are like your mother. This was Cassie's experience:

I have always had a "mother" in my life, whether it was a friend, a boss, or a boyfriend. I seem to have this incredible attraction to "motherly" types, and I know it's because my real mother wasn't there for me. But I often end up regretting my choices in people, because they often end up being just as critical and controlling of me as my mother was. I am finally learning that this attraction is based on a very childlike fantasy of getting the good mother I never had.

I've started therapy, and I find that I seem to be projecting all my "mother stuff" onto my therapist. At times I see her as all good, and I fantasize about her being my mother or my best friend. I even feel sexually attracted to her at times. At other times, though, she seems all bad to me. I start to think that she doesn't care about me at all, that it is just my money she wants. I get hurt easily if I don't think she is really listening to me. And if she seems tired or angry, I assume she is bored or angry with me. I take everything so personally. But the difference between this relationship and all my other ones is that we are working it out together. I check out my perceptions with her, and when they don't end up being right I work on not feeling like I am all bad. When my perceptions are right, my therapist acknowledges it. I'm getting more confident in my ability to trust my perceptions.

Like Cassie, the price you have paid for having someone else take care of you, dictate your life, and give you advice is that you have become dependent, childlike, resentful, lacking in self-confidence, and fearful of being alone. And, like Cassie, you probably need long-term therapy in order to heal the wounds of your childhood and to experience a positive, honest relationship. Long-term therapy provides you with a safe atmosphere in which to express all your emotions, with the safety of acceptance, and with the encouragement to own your own feelings. A good therapist can give you some of what you didn't get as a child and help you let go of your fantasy of getting a good mother. She can help you to stop seeing yourself and others as either all good or all bad, and she can help you to stand on your own, recognize your emotions, and express them without fear of rejection.

Advice to the Pleaser

Pleasers have a hard time acknowledging their own anger, pettiness, selfishness, and bitchiness. They are so bent on pleasing others that they ignore their own needs, and as a result these needs become enormous. Begin to please yourself instead of others, to acknowledge your own needs instead of having your radar out for the needs of others. Allow yourself to be bitchy, selfish, and petty at times. It will feel good. Allow yourself to get angry when your needs aren't met. One of my clients who was working hard on allowing herself to think of herself first said, "If people are going to think I am a bitch for thinking of myself first, for demanding respect from others, then they'll just have to think it!"

Many pleasers benefit from assertiveness training, which helps them learn to say no and to stand up for themselves when others put the pressure on.

Advice to the Sinner

No one deserves to be treated poorly, no matter what they've done—or think they've done—in the past. You have a tremendous amount of guilt, shame, and self-loathing, and you have probably done nothing to warrant these feelings.

Learn to differentiate between real guilt and neurotic guilt. Neurotic guilt is what you have when you feel guilty rather than accepting that you were helpless as a child, when you have taken on the guilt or shame of the person who victimized you, or when you have withheld your anger and turned it inward on yourself. If you have done any of these things, you will need to work on finding ways of constructively releasing your anger. Enter individual or group therapy, or some type of body therapy such as bioenergetics, or Reichian therapy, in which anger release is encouraged.

Real guilt, on the other hand, is your conscience's way of preventing you from doing things you will later regret or that are against society's rules. We feel real guilt when we have violated our own moral code and gone against our own value and belief systems.

Make a list of all the things you have done in your life that you feel have been wrong or hurtful to others. As you look over your list, make a distinction between those things you did as a child and those that you have done as an adult. When you were a child, you could not be held completely responsible for your actions. You were not always acting out of free choice—and in any case, since your value and belief systems were not even fully developed, you were not fully aware of the consequences of your actions.

In addition, you will need to forgive yourself for the things you did as a consequence of the childhood abuse you sustained. You may have acted out your hurt and anger by hurting yourself or others. Unable to express your anger toward your original abusers, you may have vented your anger at those who were smaller or weaker than you.

As an adult, however, you *are* responsible for your actions. For hurtful things you have done as an adult, you will need to make amends before you can truly forgive yourself. If at all possible, make some kind of contact with those you have hurt or damaged and apologize to them for your actions. You may do this in person, in a letter, or by telephone. If necessary, make restitution to the person you have hurt. If the person you hurt needs therapy because of your actions, offering to pay for his or her therapy can be an excellent way of making restitution.

If you are a religious person, pray to God for forgiveness, and then recognize that if God can forgive you then you must forgive yourself. Talk to your priest or minister about the things that you feel guilty about. He or she will be able to help you forgive yourself.

If you continue to have a difficult time forgiving yourself, you may need to seek individual therapy. Sometimes our guilt feelings are caused by deeper problems that need to be uncovered by a professional therapist.

Advice to the Victim

People don't take you seriously because you don't take yourself seriously. As you have already learned, the more you allow someone to abuse you, the less he will respect you, which in turn will encourage him to abuse you further.

There are several things that victims have in common: low self-esteem, pent-up anger, and feelings of helplessness. Continue to work on building up your self-esteem by entering individual or group therapy or by learning assertiveness. Work on the constructive release of anger by entering bioenergetics therapy, Reichian therapy, or some other type of body therapy. Every victim is secretly seething with rage at having been victimized. Unless you find some constructive release for this rage, you will continue to turn it against yourself, causing your self-esteem to continually be damaged and your self-hatred to grow.

Support groups are particularly beneficial for victims. In a support group you will learn that you are not alone, you will be encouraged to release your anger toward those who have hurt you, and you will learn that there is hope for recovery as you witness others moving forward out of their victimization. There are support groups and Twelve-Step programs for virtually every kind of victimization problem. Refer to the reference section at the back of the book for some of these listings.

It has often been said by abusers that they can spot a victim a mile away. Convicted rapists often say that they deliberately pick women who don't look assertive or strong, who they assume will not fight them off. Assertiveness-training classes and self-defense classes will help you to look, walk, and act more assertively and thus discourage abusers from seeing you as an easy target.

Advice to the Codependent

First and foremost, you will need to begin to understand that it's not your job to fix or take care of other people. Even though you have probably lived most of your life doing just that, you will now need to work on channeling your energies in other directions—most notably, in your own direction.

Until now, you have successfully managed to avoid yourself and your own problems by focusing on others. One of the reasons you have focused on others so much is that you have felt defective and flawed. You grew up believing that you mattered only through helping others. Since you haven't had control of yourself, you have tried to control others.

These buried feelings are what you need to focus on now—your feelings of shame and guilt, your feelings of worthlessness and inadequacy, your fear of being out of control. Whenever you find yourself beginning to rescue someone else, make the assumption that it is *you* whom you should be rescuing. Whenever you feel like giving someone else advice, try taking that advice yourself. And whenever you feel sorry for someone else, try feeling sorry for yourself instead.

Continue to work on connecting with your inner child, for in so doing you will be able to connect with your pain from the past. Comfort and nurture your inner child, and begin to give to her what you have given only to others in the past.

Your work on yourself needs to be your top priority right now. Attend meetings of CODA (Codependents Anonymous) or Al-Anon (for loved ones of alcholics or drug addicts) regularly, join "Women Who Love Too Much" support groups, or begin individual therapy. In addition, you might also want to read any of a number of good books about codependency (see the recommended reading section at the end of this book).

Those of you who are single will probably need to avoid entering a new romantic relationship for a while. Until you have worked on your own recovery for quite some time, you will only continue to repeat your pattern of getting involved with those who are needy, in trouble, addicted, or who cannot love you in return.

At first it will be difficult for you to be attracted to nice men. In the past you've been attracted to men whom you have wanted to change or mold into what you wanted them to be. You've always fallen in love with a man's potential instead of with who he already is. Before you get too deeply involved with anyone again, you will need to ask yourself, "Is this person meeting my needs right now?"

Those of you who are in a relationship will also need to ask yourself whether your partner is meeting your needs right now instead of expecting him to change. You will need to work on taking care of your own needs first, allowing your partner to satisfy some of your needs instead of depending only on yourself all the time, and not avoiding your own issues and problems by focusing on those of your partner.

Advice to the Drama Junkie

Because you are so used to drama, chaos, and crises, it will take some time for you to get used to peacefulness and calm. As you become healthier, you may go through a period of time when you fear that the "bubble will burst" or the "other shoe will drop" and things will go back to the way they used to be. You may also have the fear that since things have been getting better, you are somehow going to be punished or will have to pay for it. It takes time to accept the idea that you don't have to "pay" for feeling good. You deserve to have all the good feelings it's possible for a person to have, and it's time to let yourself feel good.

If you find yourself with an increasing desire to "stir things up" or initiate a crisis, it may be because things have been getting better and you are simply not used to it. It may also be the case that you need to find new channels for your need for excitement. In her book *The Agony of It All: The Drive for Drama and Excite-*

ment in *Women's Lives*, Joy Davidson proposes the theory that women are not given enough permission for excitement or provided enough constructive outlets for it. Instead, they seek excitement through their relationships, which can set them up to continually seek men who are unavailable or rejecting. Learn to get your excitement in constructive ways. Some recovering drama junkies have taken up sports such as skydiving, mountain climbing, or skiing to help quench their thirst for excitement. Others have channeled their energies into their careers, starting new businesses or entering careers that hold a great deal of challenge and excitement.

GETTING USED TO HEALTHY RELATIONSHIPS

It is natural to be afraid of change, no matter how positive the change is. We are used to the familiar, to the old ways of doing things. It can take a lot of adjusting to get used to healthy relationships.

My client Erin recently told me,

> I am very uncomfortable with the new man I am involved with. He takes me out to fancy restaurants and spends lots of money on me. I've never had a man treat me so well. He brings me flowers and treats me with respect and consideration. I'm afraid I'm going to sabotage it somehow. I'm just not used to being treated well by men. I find I have a need to control and fix somebody, and this man doesn't have any problems for me to fix.

This reminded me of something I had said to my own therapist after we had had a confrontation:

> I don't know if I'd recognize a healthy relationship if I saw one. I'm not used to being listened to when I make a request. I am used to people being defensive when I have a complaint. And I'm not used to someone actually changing a behavior so as not to hurt me.

Because of the emotional abuse that you have sustained, it is difficult for you to believe that there are, indeed, others who can meet your needs, and that you deserve to have your needs met. When our first connections are unreliable or abusive, we tend to transfer that experience onto what we expect from our friends, our mates, our coworkers, our bosses, and even our children. We expect to be abandoned, to be betrayed, to be refused, to be disappointed.

Mona came into my office with her new husband, Phil. They had been married only two months, but the marriage was already in trouble. While Mona had numerous complaints about her husband, the bottom line was that she wasn't sure that he loved her. On their second visit, Mona was particularly upset. Her hands were shaking, and she began crying almost immediately when she sat down. She told me that Phil had flirted with a waitress at a coffee shop and also with her best friend. She was also angry because she felt that he ignored her when they went out to dinner with his children from an earlier marriage. She felt he was deliberately trying to humiliate her, that he was ashamed of her, and that he was turned on to these other women. While Phil acknowledged that he had developed some bad habits in his single days, he denied having any bad intentions.

As the session progressed, I asked Mona whether any of this reminded her of anything else, either incidents from her childhood or experiences with other men. She said that as a matter of fact, her parents had been very emotionally abusive, even though they had told her that they loved her. She had learned to trust what people did rather than what they said. She said that her ex-husband had flirted with other women and had gone out on her, and that he had been ashamed of her and would ignore her in the presence of her sister-in-law.

It was difficult to determine whether Mona's perceptions about Phil were true, or whether she was just assuming that he was going to treat her in the same way that her parents and ex-husband had. As it turned out, the latter was the case. Even though Phil made sure he didn't look at other women and that he paid attention to Mona when they were around other people, she continued to come up with one complaint after another about Phil. She was so convinced that he couldn't possibly love her that she became seriously close to pushing him away entirely. Fortunately, the two continued couple counseling and were able to build enough trust between them that Mona eventually was able to recognize that Phil really did love her.

As you continue with your recovery, you will begin to recognize people as their own unique selves instead of as mere shadows from your own past. You will be able to really hear what they are saying instead of misinterpreting their words. And you will be able to take in their love instead of pushing it away, negating it, or being suspicious of it.

It can be very painful to receive genuine love. Because we are so used to being hurt and deprived, when someone gives us love that is free of expectations, criticism, and games, we can have a hard time taking it in.

And once we do begin to take in love, we may be overwhelmed with a tremendous feeling of pain. We may begin to cry and sob intensely, not being able to stop. This is because the love we are receiving reminds us of all the times we felt unloved and uncared for. Some of you are so filled up with pain that you will need to let some of the pain out to make room for the love. As painful as it is, you must make room and then allow this new, healthy love to come into you, to fill up the empty spaces inside.

Until now, you have felt that you needed to close off your heart as a protection against further hurt and betrayal. Now, it is time to start opening up your heart again—opening your heart to love.

References and Recommended Reading

EMOTIONAL CHILD ABUSE

Covitz, Joel. *Emotional Child Abuse: The Family Curse.* Boston: Sigo Press, 1986.

Miller, Alice. *Thou Shalt Not Be Aware: Society's Betrayal of the Child.* New York: New American Library, 1986.

_____. *For Your Own Good: Hidden Cruelty in Child-rearing and the Roots of Violence.* New York: Farrar Straus Giroux, 1984.

_____. *The Drama of the Gifted Child: The Search for the True Self.* New York: Basic Books, 1981.

CHILD ABUSE IN GENERAL

Farmer, Steven. *Adult Children of Abusive Parents: A Healing Program for Those Who Have Been Physically, Sexually, or Emotionally Abused.* Los Angeles: Lowell House, 1989.

Gil, Eliana. *Outgrowing the Pain: A Book for and About Adults Abused as Children.* San Francisco: Launch Press, 1983.

CHILDHOOD SEXUAL ABUSE

Bass, Ellen, and Laura Davis. *The Courage to Heal: A Guide for Women Survivors of Child Sexual Abuse.* New York: Harper & Row, 1988.

Engel, Beverly. *The Right to Innocence: Healing the Trauma of Childhood Sexual Abuse.* New York: Ballantine, 1990.

Maltz, Wendy, and Beverly Hoffman. *Incest and Sexuality: A Guide to Understanding and Healing.* Lexington, Mass.: Lexington Books, 1987.

WOMEN AS VICTIMS

Forward, Susan, and Joan Torres. *Men Who Hate Women and the Women Who Love Them.* New York: Bantam, 1986.

Dowling, Colette. *The Cinderella Complex.* New York: Summit, 1981.

Shainess, Natalie. *Sweet Suffering: Woman As Victim.* New York: Pocket Books, 1986.

YOUR INNER CHILD

Pollard, John. *Self-Parenting: The Complete Guide to Your Inner Conversations.* Malibu, Calif.: Generic Human Studies Publishing, 1987.

Whitfield, Charles. *Healing the Child Within: Discovery and Recovery for Adult Children of Dysfunctional Families.* Pompano Beach, Fla.: Health Communications, 1987.

RESOLVING RELATIONSHIPS WITH PARENTS

Bloomfield, Harold. *Making Peace with Your Parents.* New York: Ballantine, 1983.

Engel, Beverly. *Divorcing a Parent: Free Yourself From the Past and Live the Life You've Always Wanted.* Los Angeles: Lowell House, 1990.

Friday, Nancy. *My Mother/My Self.* New York: Dell Publishing, 1977.

Halpern, Howard. *Cutting Loose: An Adult Guide in Coming to Terms with Your Parents.* New York: Simon & Schuster, 1976.

Leonard, Linda Schierse. *The Wounded Woman: Healing the Father-Daughter Relationship.* Boston: Shambhala, 1985.

Viorst, Judith. *Unnecessary Losses.* New York: Ballantine, 1987.

CODEPENDENCY

Beattie, Melody. *Beyond Codependency.* San Francisco: Harper/Hazeldon, 1989.

———. *Codependent No More.* San Francisco: Harper/Hazeldon, 1987.

Norwood, Robin. *Women Who Love Too Much.* New York: Pocket Books, 1986.

Wegscheider-Cruse, Sharon. *Choice-Making: For Co-dependents, Adult Children, and Spirituality Seekers.* Pompano Beach, Fla.: Health Communications, 1985.

ADULT CHILDREN OF ALCOHOLICS

Black, Claudia. *Repeat After Me.* Denver: M.A.C. Printing, 1985.
_____. *It Will Never Happen to Me!* Denver: M.A.C. Printing, 1982.
Gravitz, Herbert, and Julie Bowden. *Guide to Recovery: A Book for Adult Children of Alcoholics.* Holmes Beach, Fla.: Learning Publications, Inc., 1985.
Woititz, Janet Geringer. *Struggle for Intimacy.* Pompano Beach, Fla.: Health Communications, 1985.
_____. *Adult Children of Alcoholics.* Pompano Beach, Fla.: Health Communications, 1983.

SELF-DISCOVERY

Capacchione, Lucia. *The Creative Journal.* Chicago: Swallow Press, 1979.
Koller, Alice. *An Unknown Woman: A Journey of Self-Discovery.* New York: Bantam, 1983.

SELF-ESTEEM

Briggs, Dorothy Corkille. *Your Child's Self-Esteem.* New York: Doubleday, 1970.
James, Jennifer. *You Know I Wouldn't Say This If I Didn't Love You: How to Defend Yourself Against Verbal Zaps and Zingers.* New York: Newmarket Press, 1990.
Phelps, Stanlee, and Nancy Austin. *The Assertive Woman: A New Look.* San Luis Obispo, Calif.: Impact Publishers, 1987.
Sanford, Linda Tschirhart, and Mary Ellen Donovan. *Women and Self-Esteem.* New York: Viking Penguin, 1985.

RELATIONSHIPS

Branden, Nathaniel. *The Psychology of Romantic Love.* New York: Bantam, 1981.

238   *References and Recommended Reading*

Lerner, Harriet. *The Dance of Anger: A Woman's Guide to Changing the Patterns of Intimate Relationships.* New York: Harper & Row, 1986.

———. *The Dance of Intimacy.* New York: Harper & Row, 1989.

Paul, Jordan, and Margaret Paul. *Do I Have to Give Up Me to Be Loved by You?* Minneapolis, MN: CompCare, 1983.

Peck, M. Scott. *The Road Less Traveled.* New York: Touchstone, 1978.

Resources

**Co-Dependents Anonymous
(CODA)**
P.O. Box 33577
Phoenix, AZ 85067
602/277-7991

**Adult Children of Alcoholics
(ACA) World Services Inc.**
P.O. Box 3216
Torrance, CA 90505
310/534-1815

**Divorcing A Parent
Workshops**
CASSA
205 Avenue I Suite 27
Redondo Beach, CA 90277
213/379-5929

**VOICES (Victims of Incest
  Can Emerge Survivors) in
Action, Inc.**
P.O. Box 148309
Chicago, IL 60614
312/327-1500

Parents Anonymous
22330 Hawthorne Blvd.
Suite 208
Torrance, CA
800/249-5506 (24-hour hotline)

**Parents United
(Daughters United/
Sons United)**
P.O. Box 952
San Jose, CA 95108
408/453-7616

**Alcoholics Anonymous World
Services, Inc.**
P.O. Box 459
Grand Central Station
New York, NY 10163
212/870-3400

**Al-Anon Family Group
Headquarters**
1372 Broadway
New York, NY 10018

Sexaholics Anonymous
P.O. Box 300
Simi Valley, CA 93062
615/331-6230

Overeaters Anonymous
World Service Office
P.O. Box 92870
Los Angeles, CA 90009
213/542-8363

Index

Abandonment, physical or emotional, 81–82

Abuse, defined, 10. *See also* Emotional abuse

Abusers. *See* Emotional abusers

Abusive expectations, 15–16, 49, 59–60

Abusive relationships. *See also* Emotional abusers; Patterns of emotional abuse
leaving versus staying in, 133–150
multiple, 94–97
original, 78–94
patterns of, 97–102
staying in, 151–177

Adult Children of Alcoholics, 104, 153–154

Agony of it All, The (Davidson), 231–232

Alcoholic parents, 84–86
adult children of, 86

Anger
of others, handling, 174
releasing, 110–115, 166–171

Antisocial personalities, 56–57, 68, 143

Assertiveness
with abusive bosses, 156, 162
learning and practicing, 7, 162–166, 230
and sexual harassment, 142

Attraction to emotional abusers, reasons for, 73–102, *See also*

Abusive relationships;
Patterns of emotional abuse

Authority figures, 7, 34, 88–90

Beattie, Melody, 40

Black, Claudia, 86

Blame, 111

Blamers, 60–61
and sinners, 67

Body, caring for, 207–208

Body memories, 110

Bosses, abusive, 7, 9, 10, 24–25, 52–53, 54–55
anger toward, 170, 172
assertiveness with, 156, 162
confronting, 141–143
female, 24–25, 59–60
mysogynists, 59–60
possessive, 50
single mothers and, 13
staying with, 154–156
when to leave, 142–143

Boundaries, establishing, 159–161, 211–213

Branden, Nathaniel, 184

Briggs, Dorothy Corkille, 223

Bulldozers, 52–53, 54, 143

Caretakers, emotionally abusive, 88–90

Chaos, constant, 19, 56–57, 98

Character assassination, 17–18, 51

Child, inner
communicating with, 127–129